li′ngō!

How to Learn a Language

Terry Doyle   Paul Meara

BBC BOOKS

This book accompanies the BBC Television programme
Lingo! How to learn a language, first broadcast on
BBC1 in September 1991.

Producer: Terry Doyle

Published by BBC Books,
a division of BBC Enterprises Limited,
Woodlands, 80 Wood Lane, London W12 0TT

First published 1991
Reprinted 1992

© Terry Doyle and Paul Meara 1991

ISBN 0 563 36275 8

Set in Linotron Plantin by Phoenix Photosetting
Printed and bound in Great Britain by
Clays Ltd, St Ives PLC.

Cover printed by
Clays Ltd, St Ives PLC.

CONTENTS

FOREWORD

This book is for anyone, anywhere, who wants to learn a language – or is maybe just thinking about it. It is written particularly with adult learners in mind: those who for reasons of pleasure, leisure, work, business or sheer curiosity, are thinking of learning a language, and are perhaps not quite sure what lies in store for them. Alternatively, if you have already started learning a language, and are experiencing difficulties of one kind or another, this book is also for you.

We have tried to tackle head-on the kinds of questions people generally ask about learning a language, and have offered some suggestions based on our own experiences, and those of a variety of adult learners across the country. There is, of course, no single best way to learn a language, and this book does not try to offer one. However, there are many ways of improving your chances of success in language-learning, and we have suggested some of these. We have illustrated them with short profiles, fictional, but based on real-life encounters between various adult learners and their chosen language – from French to Welsh, Japanese to Arabic, German to Russian. Read all of them, whatever language they deal with – they will show you how to cope with problems you might meet.

We have also tried to show something of how language works, through brief descriptions of some of the world's major languages and a summary of the degree of difficulty you might experience in learning them.

Finally, we offer you the chance to see how good you are at learning a language, through a number of quizzes or self-testing activities. We hope you'll find these fun, as well as useful. All in all, *we've* tried to provide a mine of helpful information and ideas, as well as insights into languages and how to learn them. We hope some of these will help *you* to **'learn the lingo'**.

Terry Doyle
Paul Meara

Acknowledgements

Terry Doyle would like to thank his friends and colleagues at the BBC for many years of shared ideas, discussion and debate about languages and how to learn them. He is particularly grateful to Jane Cottave for her research contribution to this book.

Paul Meara would like to thank his colleagues at University College, Swansea, and Gwenllian Awbery for their help during the writing, and his friends, relations and students who provided the inspiration for the case studies.

We would like to acknowledge the help of the Centre for Information on Language Teaching and Research, the British Council, Accelerated Learning Systems Limited, and Professor David Crystal's *Cambridge Encyclopedia of Language*.

We would also like to acknowledge a special debt to John Trim, who taught us both a lot of what we know about languages and ways of learning them.

Lingo n. colloqu. – foreign, strange or unintelligible language [prob. fr. Portuguese *lingoa* fr. Latin *lingua*: tongue]

GETTING GOING

If you're about to have a go at learning a language, or can't make up your mind whether it's worth the effort, time or expense involved, you're probably asking yourself one or more of the following questions. A few answers may help you decide whether it's worth getting going at all:

1 Why learn a language?

2 Which language?

3 How do I make a start?

4 Is it best to learn on my own, or with a teacher or group?

5 How much will it cost me?

6 How long will it take me?

7 What is a multi-media course?

8 How can I find the time?

9 Can anyone learn a language?

10 Am I too old to learn a language?

11 How much can I learn?

12 How fast can I learn?

13 What skills do I need in order to learn?

14 How many words do I need to learn?

15 Will I need to learn grammar?

16 Does my pronunciation matter?

17 What's the best method for me to follow?

18 Will I find some languages harder than others?

19 If I learn one language, does it help with learning others?

20 How do languages work?

1 Why learn a language?

Why do you want to learn a language? It's important to be clear about this from the word go. Motivation in the beginning is what will keep you going when the going gets tough. Later on, there'll be tips and hints for reinforcing motivation, maintaining the drive and will-power to overcome the obstacles, as well as advice on how to pursue the enjoyment and resist the natural temptation to give up or drop out when memory fails, or progress falters.

But why learn a language anyway? If you are a native English-speaker you could perhaps be forgiven for asking the question. After all, English is in many ways *the* world language, a lingua franca for international communication.

It is currently estimated that there are some 350 million or more people for whom English is their primary language, and over a billion more who use it as an official language. This is the legacy of the British Empire, the political and commercial influence of the United States, the charm of the cinema, the pervasive pull of pop music, the persuasive power of television and radio.

English also has many linguistic features which add to its international appeal: it is grammatically less complex than most languages, has a large vocabulary derived from Greek or Latin (making it accessible to many cultures) and is versatile and flexible, easily embracing words and concepts from other languages. It is also capable of being simplified while still remaining apparently successful as a basic means of international communication. This characteristic is giving rise to what has been called the 'New English' – international versions of the language – enabling non-native speakers to talk to each other on a superficial level.

The main reason, however, for the spread of English as an influential world language, lies not so much in its inherent characteristics (let alone 'superiority') as in the cultural, commercial, military, social and political activities of its speakers across the centuries.

English, as a result, is the main official language of the United Nations Organization, the international language of aviation (air traffic control), the specialist language of mathematics, science and computers, the popular language of commerce, travel, sports and international conferences. Of all the printed matter in the world, 50 per cent is in English. Five of the largest broadcasting companies in the world (CBS, NBC, ABC, BBC, CBC) and, in the field of non-stop

---

English is spoken as a native, official, second or cultural language in: American Samoa, Anguilla, Antigua and Barbuda, Australia, Bahamas, Barbados, Belize, Bermuda, Botswana, British Virgin Isles, Brunei, Cameroon, Canada, Cayman Isles, Christmas Islands, Cocos Islands, Cook Isles, Dominica, Falkland Isles, Fiji, Gambia, Ghana, Gibraltar, Grenada, Guam, Guernsey, Guyana, Hong Kong, India, Irish Republic, Isle of Man, Jamaica, Jersey, Kenya, Kiribati, Lesotho, Liberia, Malawi, Malta, Mauritius, Monserrat, Namibia, New Zealand, Nigeria, Niue, Norfolk Isles, Pacific Isles, Papua New Guinea, Philippines, Puerto Rico, St Christopher and Nevis, St Helena and Ascension, St Lucia, St Vincent, Seychelles, Sierra Leone, Singapore, Solomon Isles, South Africa, Surinam, Swaziland, Tanzania, Tokelau, Tonga, Trinidad and Tobago, Turks and Calcos Isles, Tuvalu, Uganda, United Kingdom, United States of America, Vanuatu, US Virgin Isles, Western Samoa, Zambia, Zimbabwe.

news coverage, CNN, transmit in English to audiences that regularly exceed 100 million.

In addition to the impressive list on page 11 many other nations in Europe, Africa and Asia, from China to the USSR, make English the first foreign language to be taught, whether for reasons of historical or linguistic affinity, or for cultural or commercial gain. This certainly accounts for at least 100 million more users.

Yet it is still true that most people in the world do not speak English, or indeed wish to speak English. In Europe, and other parts of the world, business is being carried out in several languages including English. This puts people who speak only English at a severe disadvantage in what is increasingly a multilingual market-place. Most people in the European Community don't speak English, yet many British companies remain convinced that it will always be the language of international business. In fact, in the future the true business language will be that of the client. And there are many other reasons why learning another language will repay the effort involved.

> The United Nations operates in five different languages: English, French, Russian, Chinese and Arabic.

World travel: Many more people are packing a language along with their toothbrush and trainers, and adding a new dimension to the adventure of travel.

Multilingual societies: These create a need for multicultural and multilinguistic understanding. An awareness of the nature of ethnic or 'community' languages can contribute to this understanding.

Vocational and commercial opportunities: Knowledge of another language expands these greatly. Companies who need to be competitive in the Single European Market are realising the handicaps of monolingualism (speaking only one language), and now acknowledge that if their executives

> Over 160 languages are used in Britain by ethnic minority communities. The most widely spoken immigrant languages are: Hindi, Urdu, Punjabi, Bengali, Gujarati, German, Polish, Italian, Greek, Spanish and Cantonese.

and other employees know a foreign language or two this can increase promotion prospects and be, literally, 'good for business'. In the new Europe, you improve your corporate image if you improve your language profile. After all, doing business abroad is partly about creating a relationship with people from other countries, and the best way to do that is to learn at least some of their language.

Personal enrichment: To learn another language is to expand your world view and gain a new perspective on your own language and culture. It is the first step in getting to know another people, another country, another culture from the inside, through their language.

So, whether you're a young person setting out on your first travels, a businessman with an eye on improved trading prospects, a nurse or social worker dealing with people who speak imperfect English, a family off to the Costa Brava in the summer, or a pensioner simply learning for fun, first be clear why you wish to learn a language, and what you want to do with it. What do you wish to *use* the language for?

> There are 12 countries in the European Community, and nine official working languages: English, French, German, Spanish, Italian, Dutch, Danish, Greek and Portuguese. All Community documents have to be translated into all of these languages.

2 Which language?

You may already have a firm idea of the particular language you want or need to learn: perhaps you're going to that country on holiday, for a business trip, to work, move or retire there. Or you may wish to have access to its scientific journals or its literature, its radio or satellite television programmes, its press or publicity.

Alternatively, you may simply want to learn a language that attracts you for its sound, its usefulness, its world-wide importance, its people or culture.

Whatever the reason, the choice is not always obvious.

Historically, many British people have been put off learning languages by their experience of being taught, and having to learn, French at school – all those genders, agreements, conjugations and subjunctives, and scarcely a meaningful word to show for it. Thankfully, teaching methods have improved enormously since those bad old days, and the policy now is to teach language for communication and to encourage the learning of a variety of languages in schools (though the lack of trained teachers is making this difficult).

In fact, French, though the language of our closest neighbours, and the key to one of the world's richest cultures, is not an easy language for us to learn as a first foreign language – its grammar, pronunciation and spelling pose considerable difficulties for English speakers. Italian, German or Spanish may be an easier way into language-learning and confidence-building at the beginning.

A basic knowledge of less commonly taught languages, such as Greek, Portuguese or Turkish, may be of just as much use to the holiday-maker as the more obvious choices,

---

The Council of Europe recognises 25 countries, which represent 17 languages. In addition to those of the European Community these are: Turkish, Finnish, Irish, Icelandic, Norwegian, Swedish, Hungarian, Czech. The Council's three working languages are English, French and German.

and they're not necessarily more difficult.

Great world languages, such as Russian, Arabic and Chinese, though probably not top of most people's priority list for first foreign language, may well prove the most useful or appropriate second choice. Japan's rise to economic dominance has made Japanese a more attractive, less unthinkable, less 'exotic' option for language-learning than it may have been in the past.

The world's top 12 languages

It is estimated that at least 4000 languages are spoken throughout the world! Some say as many as 10 000.

There are two basic ways of measuring how important they are.

1 According to the number of speakers using the language as their mother tongue.

2 According to the total populations of countries where the language has official status (though not everyone may speak it fluently).

The figures below should be taken as an estimated guide to current trends.

Mother-tongue speakers (millions)		*Official-language speakers (millions)*	
1 Chinese	1000	1 English	1400
2 English	350	2 Chinese	1000
3 Spanish	260	3 Hindi	700
4 Hindi	200	4 Spanish	280
5 Arabic	150	5 Russian	270
6 Bengali	150	6 French	220
7 Russian	150	7 Arabic	170
8 Portuguese	135	8 Portuguese	160
9 Japanese	124	9 Malay	160
10 German	100	10 Bengali	150
11 French	70	11 Japanese	124
12 Punjabi	70	12 German	100

What is more, one of the main stumbling-blocks to successful learning of such less commonly taught languages, namely the lack of suitable up-to-date materials, is gradually being removed as course designers apply modern communicative principles to the design of materials for languages other than English and French.

All in all, the choice of which language to learn is vast, and expanding. So weigh your options carefully and choose according to your own personal needs, interests and appetite. Throughout the book you'll find brief descriptions of some of the world's major languages (and a few minor ones, too) to help you make up your mind.

3 How do I make a start?

We all learn in different ways, and what's right for one learner may not be right for another. When making a start, find ways to suit yourself – your needs, your interest, your personal circumstances, your pocket. If it works for you, that's fine.

Start by checking out the classes in your local school, college of further education, polytechnic, or university extramural centre and see if there's one at your level. Choose a course and a course book which feel right for you: the right style, the right contents, the right level. Take the advice of a teacher or course tutor. Clarify with him or her your goals and objectives, your likely level of achievement and the commitment you'll be expected to make over and above the classes if you're to make real progress. Check out the opportunities for studying by yourself, the degree of flexibility with which you'll be able to organise your own study timetable, to fit in with your own requirements.

If there's no class available and if, for that or any other reason, you decide to learn at home by yourself, the most important decision you'll face is which course book to use

(p. 174). If you can, choose one with accompanying audio cassettes.

So, you've found your course. You're ready to go.

Here are a few **do's** and **don'ts** that will help you make the most of it:

★ **Do** have a go: it's important to aim for the best pronunciation you can, but

★ **Don't** clam up just because you think your accent's not perfect. Like so many aspects of language-learning, it will improve with practice.

★ **Do** spend lots of time listening, and try to spot the difference between the sounds of English and the sounds of your new language.

★ **Don't** be tempted to work from the printed page and pronounce the foreign language as if it were English.

★ **Do** listen to good models and try to reproduce the sounds as closely as you can. If there's not enough opportunity for you to practise in class, try to spend time in a language laboratory working on your own.

★ **Do** choose a course which lays the stress on communication and using the language.

★ **Don't** be put off by grammar.

★ **Don't** worry if it seems that there isn't enough grammar. It is there all right, whether you like it or not. It may simply be that your course, or your teacher, is choosing not to draw attention to grammar at that point, but is presenting it through an activity or an example instead. It's sometimes easier and more useful to understand a point of grammar once you've seen and heard it used in a particular context or situation. And, if you really must know, you can always look it up in the reference section which most good course books provide.

★ **Don't** try to go too fast at the beginning, but

★ **Do** keep revising what you've already learnt. When you learn a new structure or piece of vocabulary, try to use it straight away – and then again and again. There are various techniques for memorising vocabulary, and we'll go into these later (p. 83), but for the moment remember that *using* a word or phrase is the best way to fix it in your memory.

★ **Don't** get disheartened if, after early signs of progress in the first flush of enthusiasm, you seem to slow down. This is normal. Language-learning has peaks and troughs. There are moments when your pronunciation is spot on, your vocabulary seemingly inexhaustible, your grammar impeccable, your powers of communication quite eloquent; and others when you can't remember the most obvious word, make the silliest of mistakes and can't pronounce a thing. Be patient! And keep going.

4 Is it best to learn on my own, or with a teacher or group?

Learning a language is a two-way process. However you go about it, you have to learn consciously how the language works and you have to use it to communicate. The basic aim is usually to talk to other people, so the process may be more enjoyable, and in some ways more effective, if you can do it with a group, a class or a teacher.

There are other advantages to learning with a group. The social aspect can be very good for motivation, and it helps to see that others experience the same anxieties, queries, mistakes and failures – as well as successes! – as you do. It's also invaluable to have a good teacher to guide you through the process of language-learning, explaining things, providing a model, monitoring your mistakes, assessing your progress, encouraging you when the going gets tough, sharing their own experience of the language and its culture and their enthusiasm for it.

However, it may not be convenient for you to learn with a group or teacher. There may be no class near your home or work; there may not be a class or teacher in the language of your choice (this is particularly the case with less commonly taught languages such as Portuguese, Greek or Japanese); the class may have already started and be in full swing by the time you decide you want to start learning. Even if you do manage to join a class, there are disadvantages. You may be forced to proceed at the pace of the group as a whole, and this could be either too fast or too slow for you; there may not be enough opportunity for you to practise speaking the language if the class is a big one; if you miss a lesson or two you'll feel left behind and be tempted to give up.

So there are advantages, too, in learning by yourself, at least for a good part of the time. You can organise your own timetable (p. 27); take part fully in a learning process defined only by yourself and your chosen course; proceed at your own pace; learn what and how much you want, in the way that suits you at the time that suits you, in the place that suits you. There's no competition (this can work both ways!), no time pressure other than that which you set yourself, no one to hear your mistakes or grimace at your pronunciation or accent.

In any case, most of the real learning takes place when you're by yourself. It's the work you do on your own between classes that helps you progress and benefit fully from them.

Publishers and broadcasters have come to the aid of the person studying a language on their own at home. In the past, many courses assumed the presence of a teacher and a classroom. Today, there is a huge range of broadcast multi-media courses (p. 23), correspondence courses, 'distance learning' programmes and cassette courses designed for individual home learning. As far as materials are concerned, it has never been easier to learn a language on your own. Making the effort and maintaining the necessary discipline are other matters, of course, and we'll show you how to do that in the sections that follow.

So, is it best to learn on my own or in a group? The answer is: it depends very much on your circumstances and inclinations. If you can do both, so much the better. If you have to choose one or the other, remember that there are advantages and disadvantages to both. In the end, the progress you'll make will depend on you taking responsibility for, and pride in, your own learning. That's where the greatest satisfaction lies.

5 How much will it cost me?

An evening class run by your local education authority is a very reasonably priced way to learn a language, and good value for money. You can expect to pay about £22 per 10-week term for the classes. You'll also have to buy your course book, but it may be possible to share audios, videos and other materials with other students in the class.

Course books vary in price. At the cheap end of the market, a basic *Get By In* . . . course costs from £2.95 for the book only, and from £10.95 for the book and the accompanying audio cassettes. And the radio (or television) programme won't cost you anything – once you've paid your licence fee.

At the other end of the scale, a suggestopaedic course (p. 32) in a foreign language can cost upwards of £6000 for 60 hours tuition. These courses are tailor-made for groups of company executives and take account of the language-learning, social and business needs of individuals and the company. They are organised and arranged to suit the working timetables of the participants and proceed at an intensive pace, applying the full gamut of techniques available to this particular method (relaxation, music, games, role-playing, dual-language texts and tapes, dramatic reading, etc.).

And, of course, between these two extremes there is an enormous variety of published courses – books with or without cassettes and other materials – at prices to suit every pocket.

Individual tuition on an intensive or 'crash course' basis is one of the most expensive ways of learning a language, though some people find it very effective. Major language schools charge something like £30 or £40 an hour (or 45-minute period) depending on the language. (These and other prices quoted here were correct at the time of going to press.) The recommended number of hours tuition varies from language to language, and depends on your language-learning experience and aptitude. And yes, some languages are more expensive than others: Japanese is notoriously expensive, and Arabic is not cheap either. You don't need to go to a commercial language school to learn a language intensively, however. Many universities, polytechnics, colleges and local authorities run intensive courses at more accessible prices.

Later in the book (p. 174) you'll find some tips on how to select the course that suits you – method-wise and price-wise too.

So, how much will it cost me to learn a language? The answer is: you should be able to find something that will fit any budget.

6 How long will it take me?
It all depends.

★ It depends on how motivated you are. If you have, for example, a deadline by which you know you must be able to cope with the language – a family holiday, for instance, a business trip abroad, an examination you want to take to gain a qualification – you'll pace yourself in order to reach that goal. Having a concrete reason for learning a language is also a sound basis for success.

★ It depends on the amount of time and energy you are prepared to devote to the task, and what kind of learner you are (p. 46).

★ Finally, it depends which native tongue you start from and which 'target' language you plan to learn: whether it's a Germanic language (p. 51), a Romance language (p. 63), a

Slavic language (p. 110) or a non-Indo-European language such as Japanese (p. 87). If your target language is in the same family as your native one, learning will be easier and faster since there are many 'instant connections' to be made between the two in terms of vocabulary, grammar and even pronunciation. If your target language is from a completely different language family, and has, for example, a different script, you'll need to allow that much more time for successful mastery.

A Dutch speaker, for instance, finds it easier to learn German than a French speaker; a Portuguese finds it easier to learn Spanish than an English speaker.

English speakers are very fortunate in that the English language has Germanic and Latin connections, giving easier access to both the Germanic- and the Romance-language families.

If:

★ your motivation is strong

★ your aptitude is reasonable

★ you are able to devote sufficient regular time to learning the language (p. 27)

★ your native language is English and your target language is either Germanic (German, Dutch or Danish, for example) or Romance (French, Spanish, Italian or Portuguese)

Then:

You will need about **120 hours** of study to achieve a reasonable degree of competence in understanding and speaking the language. So, if you work steadily and regularly for **5 hours a week** you can expect to have made some real progress in about **6 months**.

Of course, it is possible to learn something in a month, a week, a day, an hour even. If you are able to spare the time to learn more intensively, and increase the number of hours study per week, your total learning period may be reduced. Learning intensively is also good for self-confidence, since

Intensive-language-training schools recommend the following exposure for English speakers beginning a language:

French, Italian, Spanish, Portuguese	255 hours
Dutch, German, Scandinavian	285 hours
Greek	330 hours
Russian	330 hours
Arabic	375–420 hours
Japanese	375–420 hours

Europeans learning English from scratch can expect to spend 270 hours, and a Japanese learning English between 360 and 450 hours.

you are more aware of making quick progress. On the other hand, quickly learned may be quickly forgotten. It should, in any case, be recognised that language-learning, once begun, is a lifelong process, and that the 6-month target suggested above represents a beginning, by no means an end! Fluency, of course, takes a lot longer.

7 What is a multi-media course?

At its most basic, the term 'multi-media' simply means using more than one medium for teaching or learning. In this sense, a teacher and a book constitute a multi-media course, since a good teacher is a medium for learning. Mostly, however, the term is used to indicate a language course which contains a variety of media including, usually, a broadcast component: television or radio, or both. In addition to the course book, courses like these may also incorporate audio cassettes, notes for teachers wishing to exploit the courses in the classroom, video packs.

Television and radio courses have one obvious advantage in common: they are free, or at least very cheap! All you have to do is make an appointment with the broadcast or transmission time, and there you are, transported to the country, listening to the language, meeting the people, absorbing the sights and sounds of another culture – all in your own living-room! And, of course, audio- and video-recording techniques make this process even easier.

Television and radio courses are designed specifically with the person learning on their own at home in mind, though you're also encouraged to join a group or a class using the same course if at all possible.

So, if you're learning on your own at home, what can you expect to get out of the different components of a multi-media course?

A good course will encourage you to use the language right from the start.

One designed for beginners will normally aim to take you up to a stage where you can communicate at a basic level, in a variety of everyday situations, in the language of your choice. This will involve the skills of listening, speaking, understanding, reading and, sometimes, writing. In fact, writing things down is a very useful way of fixing new words in your head, and revising them when they begin to fade away!

Television programmes are, of course, a prime motivator. They're what get hundreds of thousands, sometimes millions, of people interested in learning the language in the first place. Whether they use documentary film or dramas, cartoon animation or electronic graphics, 'vox pop' (Latin *vox populi* – 'voice of the people') interviews or on-the-spot reportage, they can convey the look of the place, the feel of the people, the sound of the language, the interest of the culture – everything except the smell!

At their best, they can make a foreign language and a

foreign culture accessible in a way in which no other medium can. They demonstrate the feasibility of learning the language, the doors it opens to the culture, the hand it stretches out to another people.

But, though it can do all these things, a television programme on its own can't teach you to speak a language. It may help you to develop your understanding of both the language and the culture and, when used imaginatively as a video, may help promote active listening and creative use of vocabulary and structures. It may also be used to stimulate controlled dialogue about the cultural content of the programme. But it still won't teach you to speak the language.

Radio programmes focus more exclusively on sound. Most radio courses give you lots of chances to practise the language through exercises, and opportunities to listen to a wide variety of different voices.

Audio cassettes are a key medium for developing the skills of listening and speaking. Flexible in their use – in the bath, in the car, on a bus or bicycle – they are the best way to attune your ear to how the language sounds (intonation, pronunciation, rhythm, accent) and allow you to practise your imitations in privacy. They provide models for pronunciation, dialogues to listen to and take part in and exercises to try out the patterns and structures of the language explained in the book.

They may be used with the book, or without, depending on how closely integrated the two media are.

The book itself is usually the core of the course. Though course books vary in style and content, each unit will invariably contain a number of predictable features:

★ A small number of **key structures** or patterns for you to focus on.

★ **Examples** of these structures used in realistic, sometimes completely authentic, dialogues recorded on location in the country.

★ **Glossary notes** explaining new vocabulary and idioms (turns of phrase peculiar to the language, usually untranslatable in a literal sense).

★ **Notes on** aspects of the **culture** of the country. It's always important to understand the cultural context in which the language you're learning is used by native speakers.

★ **Grammatical explanations** where appropriate, though these are now more commonly reserved for a reference section you can turn to when you feel the need for them.

★ Opportunities for you to try out the language you've learnt in the form of **exercises** or puzzles.

★ **Summary sections** that give you the chance to assess your progress or revise anything you may have forgotten.

Most course designers will recommend that you study the materials in a multi-media course 'little and often' – better half an hour a day than 3 hours once a week. This holds true for all language-learning. Add to this patience, persistence and practice, and you'll find that your understanding and your ability to speak will improve – sometimes beyond all expectation!

However much language you learn, when you go to the country you'll inevitably find yourself in a situation where you're surrounded by more language (a lot more!) than you can handle. You have to learn to guess a little what's going on – from the context or situation you're in, from the relationships between the people who are speaking, from visual clues, body language ('non-verbal behaviour' in the jargon), tone of voice – and by listening out for words you do know and can recognise (there will always be some!). These all act as hooks you can peg your general understanding on. You will rarely be able to understand every word. Some courses try to prepare you for just this eventuality, and you'll often be told: 'Don't expect to understand every word.' This can be frustrating, since our natural inclination is to do just that, but it's none the less good advice. Learn to listen for the 'gist' of what's going on, and fill the details in later. Television and video, with their in-built visual support, are particularly good at helping you develop such 'gist understanding'.

New technologies are constantly being developed and can become part of the language-learner's repertoire. Satellite television provides an unlimited linguistic and cultural resource. Microcomputers can take a lot of the drudge out of language-learning, especially when it comes to reading, writing and consolidating vocabulary or structures. Interactive video combines the limitless logic and patience of the computer with the rich audio-visual context of video, all under the individual control of the learner, who can proceed and progress entirely at his or her own pace.

Certainly, as we head towards the year 2000, there's no shortage of media that can be used to learn a language – and never was the need so great!

8 How can I find the time?

It's important to organise and manage your time so that you regularly expose yourself in different ways to different aspects of the language you're learning.

Make a regular and consistent date with your language, and don't stand it up!

If you're studying with a teacher, one to one, or in a class, that's one regular appointment you'll need to keep. Missing it could put you on the slippery slope to falling behind and eventually dropping out. If you're studying on your own, the appointment is with yourself. Sometimes this is even harder to keep! If you're doing a multi-media course, you can use the different components to help you structure your learning in, say, 1-week blocks, with each block containing a series of appointments.

Appointment 1: Watch TV programme — ½ hour

Appointment 2: Work through corresponding
unit in course book — 1½ hours

Appointment 3: Listen to corresponding unit on
audio cassettes — 1 hour

Appointment 4: Listen to corresponding radio
programme *or* review audio-cassette material — ½ hour

Appointment 5: Review course-book material;
focus on practice of language studied — 1 hour

Appointment 6: Watch repeat of television
programme/review on video if available — ½ hour

Total: 5 hours

Make learning your language a priority. Try to keep these appointments at the same specific times each week. Put them in your diary. Use them to monitor your own progress. One of the advantages of learning by yourself is that you can be self-scheduling: you can learn what *you* want to learn, *how* and *when* you want to learn. The above schedule is just one suggestion. Perhaps a different one will work for you. The important thing is to fix your own schedule and stick to it.

In brief, the answer to the question, 'How can I find the time?' is: make the time!

9 Can anyone learn a language?

Different people have different aptitudes for learning a foreign language. This depends to a degree on your style of learning. While some people are good at, say, memorising vocabulary, others find pronunciation easy. Some may find it relatively easy to communicate in their chosen language, but find it hard to grasp grammatical concepts in the abstract. Some people are good at all these things, others have to work hard at them.

But we all can learn a language. The fact that we all learned our mother tongue is one proof of this. The fact that very few cultures in the world are monolingual (in most cultures more than one language is spoken on a daily basis) is another.

The British are no exception. As we've seen, the international spread of English has perhaps led to some rather lazy attitudes towards learning other people's languages. However, as a nation, the British are no better or worse at learning languages than anyone else. We simply haven't bothered much and, as a result, it's not as much part of our culture as it is in some other countries.

Learning a second foreign language as an adult is a different experience from learning your native language as a child. For one thing, as a child you spend much longer at it (some say as much as 5000 hours on average); for another, you are constantly surrounded by the language with, usually, at least one permanent teacher on call, constantly stimulating, reinforcing, correcting your every utterance and, frequently, marvelling at your linguistic ability and achievement. This is very good for self-confidence, one of the prime elements in successful language-learning! But this total immersion, however intensive the course, can never be quite reproduced in adult life. And there's another factor. Even if you are resident in the country of your target language, your native language is always there to interfere with your learning of the foreign one: you have a natural inclination to transfer the automatic habits of grammar, vocabulary, accent, pronunciation and native-language idioms picked up in childhood to your foreign language. This has to be consciously avoided by the adult learner, whereas a child has no such interference to beware of.

But there are also bonuses to being an adult learner!

10 Am I too old to learn a language?
Although early childhood is in many ways the best time for

learning languages, it is nevertheless true that you're never too old to learn. In fact, learning something new in later life, especially a language, actually helps to keep the brain in trim. Your brain continues to develop and function more efficiently through the stimulation. You may not find it quite so easy to achieve perfect pronunciation, since in most people the ability to mimic reaches its peak in childhood. Your short-term memory may not be as good as it was. But these handicaps are balanced by your capacity to understand and acquire the new concepts essential to learning a language. You will be able to spot and transfer patterns in the new one, making learning easier. You will, with a little effort, be able to overcome the notion that other languages work (or *should* work) in precisely the same way your own language works. You will learn to accept the target language on its own terms – the first step towards knowing and accepting the culture on its own terms. This may even cause you to reflect upon, and see in a different perspective, your own language and culture. And this is no bad thing.

Adults, therefore, have an advantage over children in that they are able to bring understanding of language, and indeed life experience, to the learning of a foreign language, and can build new language structures and cultural awareness on this understanding. They are more able to see that learning a language is the key to another culture. This adds to their motivation, and helps them to learn.

If you're retired, you are more able to give priority to your language-learning. You have the advantage of being able to go at your own pace and learn in your own time. You'll find it easier to keep to the 'appointment system' for successful learning outlined earlier. There are many cases of retired people who have started learning a language as complete beginners and, 2 or 3 years later, passed 'A' level with flying colours.

So, am I too old to learn a language? The answer is very simple: no!

11 How much can I learn?

It's important to be realistic about your goals, objectives and progress. Above all, set yourself achievable targets. Learn and review a reasonable set number of words each day (20 or so should be a maximum). Give yourself the weekly goal of not only, say, completing a unit of your course book, but also being able to do something with the language: something basic, such as being able to order a drink in a café or bar, introduce yourself to someone or ask the way in the street. This way, you'll be building up a kind of personal credit system of functions you can progressively perform in the language. Instead of regarding total fluency at some point in the dim and distant future as your aim, pile up these small achievements one by one, step by step, revising as you go. Failure to achieve total fluency in a fortnight does *not* mean you are incapable of learning a language. Just keep building up your deposits in your credit bank of achievement. You will see the interest growing, and be confident that the investment will eventually pay off.

And when you achieve your set target, reward yourself. A bottle of wine, a day of leisure, a night out perhaps.

Many people drop out of language courses after the first flush of enthusiasm has waned: they may miss a class or two, miss an appointment with one or more of the broadcast programmes, even miss appointments with themselves. They may feel they are not making progress fast enough, or have just 'got stuck'. Discouragement sets in. The result – drop-out. Setting yourself realistic targets – reasonable chunks you can handle – and managing your time effectively, are two ways of combating drop-out. If you've fallen behind, find someone – a teacher, a native speaker, a friend, neighbour or relative – who can help you catch up. If you feel like giving up: don't! Keep going. The advantages of sticking with it far outweigh the temporary set-backs that every learner of a foreign language experiences. One simple way of restoring your self-confidence when the going gets tough is to go back to an earlier unit, and see how easy it seems! That way, you'll convince yourself that you are indeed capable of further progress. Try visualising yourself as a successful user of the language in the situation of your choice – making friends, having a good time, enjoying a holiday, clinching a business deal. Such positive images will reinforce your self-image as a successful language-learner, and combat any doubts you may have that you can do it.

One answer to the question, 'How much can I learn?' is: don't try and learn too much! That way, you'll learn as much as you need to at each stage of the process.

12 How fast can I learn?

Most people think that learning a language is a long, slow, painful, time-consuming activity. It is actually a lifelong process, not something that starts and then stops when you've got to the end. We are continuously adding to our knowledge of our own native language. The same is true of a foreign language. None the less, for as long as there have been language-learners there have been attempts to find easier, faster, quicker, more painless ways of learning. Publishers of language-course books have not been slow to suggest the quick fix with titles like, 'French without Tears', 'Japanese in a Week', 'Thai in Three Months', 'Learn French, German, Spanish or Italian in 3½ weeks', etc.

There is no doubt that there are ways to make certain aspects of language-learning more enjoyable and more effective – and therefore faster. Recent decades have seen a proliferation of theories, techniques, approaches and systems designed to improve our ability to learn all kinds of things, and language-learning has been at the centre of these experiments: sleeplearning, suggestology, Suggestopaedia, mindmapping, Inner Track learning, Neuro-Linguistic Programming, Superlearning, left brain–right brain theory, and, most recently, Accelerated Learning.

Such approaches and materials are based on two fundamental principles:

1 Presentation of the foreign language in a way which appeals to the visual, auditory and physical senses of the learner.
2 Active and deliberate involvement of both the left and right sides of the brain so that the emotions are included in the learning process.

One of the pioneers in the field, the Bulgarian scientist Dr Georgi Lozanov, showed that a combination of relaxation techniques and certain kinds of music could help to maximise the hidden potential of the brain and thus speed up the learning process. These discoveries were linked to research into the brain which showed that its two halves ('left' and 'right') function in different, though complementary ways: the left brain deals mainly with logic, analysis, words and step-by-step presentation, whereas the right brain deals more with patterns, images, imagination, rhythm and 'getting the overall picture'.

Many traditional language-teaching methods and materials focused almost exclusively on what the left brain is good at: the cool, logical, theoretical, analytical (grammar-translation) approach. Approaches based on techniques such as accelerated learning set out deliberately to engage and involve both sides of the brain, and therefore include the emotions. We learn and remember more effectively (especially long term) if our emotions are involved – hence the use of music.

We also learn more effectively if all our senses are engaged in the learning process. Some of us are primarily visual learners, some more 'auditory' (we learn better through sound). Others are more 'kinaesthetic' and learn better through doing things, being 'involved'. Most of us are a mixture of all three, and proponents of approaches and materials designed for these learning styles are convinced they can improve our ability to assimilate and retain a foreign language, and accelerate the speed at which we do so.

Characteristics of courses designed to speed up learning by engaging all the senses include: relaxation, use of the imagination, peripheral vision (taking in dual-language texts subconsciously), an involving story-line, memory maps, games and, not least, music, especially baroque music.

Some people have found that approaches like these work faster than other methods of teaching and they might be right for you. Anyone trying them has to make an extra effort to apply the discipline of the method in addition to that of language-learning itself, and this can be too much for some people. However, for many it's a discipline which brings its own rewards in the form of enjoyable and effective learning.

So, how fast can you learn? The answer is: faster than you think if you find a course that suits your style of learning.

13 What skills do I need in order to learn?

Using a language means:

★ speaking
★ listening
★ reading
★ writing

These in turn mean acquiring a good pronunciation, understanding grammar and syntax (the way the language works), building up and memorising vocabulary and mastering the idiom of the language.

Many physiological and psychological, as well as linguistic, processes are involved in acquiring these skills. Speaking involves a variety of motor skills, and quite complex manipulation of the muscles in your throat and mouth. Understanding involves developing the additional skill of listening for meaning, as well as simply hearing sounds accurately enough to reproduce them. Reading means recognising words and the links between them, and relating these to the sounds of the words when spoken. Writing means reproducing accurately and in detail the phonetic and semantic content of the language – what it sounds like, what it looks like and what it means. No mean feat!

Traditional language-teaching emphasised reading and writing, frequently at the expense of the ability to speak and understand. Such teaching told you a lot about the language, but didn't give you much chance to communicate in it. There was much analysis of grammar, much emphasis on translation both from and into the target language, much correcting of anything other than the perfect utterance. This kind of approach might have suited academic learners, but made it look as though learning was pretty hard (and pretty boring!) and could be done only if you were really brainy!

Times have changed, radically. Language-teaching today stresses the ability to communicate first and foremost – and, above all, this usually means listening and speaking. This is not to say that the skills of reading and writing are no longer important. Quite the opposite. Reading (newspapers and magazines, for example – it doesn't have to be the classical literature of the country in question!) is one of the best ways of increasing your vocabulary. Writing words and phrases down, for example in your vocabulary book, is an excellent way of improving your memory. It helps you to remember the shapes of words and phrases.

As well as these fundamental language skills, there are a number of other skills you may wish to add to your language-learning armoury:

★ Develop a **learning rhythm** which takes you, in order, from listening to speaking to reading to writing. In the first instance, this sequence will improve your pronunciation. Secondly, it will reinforce your understanding and learning and, thirdly, it will help to fix words and phrases in your short-term memory. If you prefer, speaking and reading may be reversed or practised at the same time.

★ Cultivate the habit of **learning in chunks**: memorising long lists of isolated words is neither an interesting nor an effective way of building your vocabulary. It is far better to learn sentences, phrases or structures that contain useful words and are in a meaningful context.

★ Expose yourself to constant **repetition**, from a variety of sources. Repetition is boring unless it is varied, so make full use of different media (television, video, radio, audio, language laboratory, computers, magazines, newspapers) to review and revise language learned.

★ **Involve** yourself as fully as possible in both learning and practising – with languages, to practise is to learn. The key is not to be shy (it's well established that learning another language can contribute substantially to personality growth, extending your personality into unknown territories). Don't be afraid to talk out loud, mistakes and all; to record your voice and re-record until you're satisfied your accent's improving; to act out whatever dialogues you're working on. If you really want to learn another language you have to make the effort, at some point, to get under the skin of the other culture. The most effective language-learners are those who develop empathy with (or a feeling for) the other language and the other people, and make the leap of imagination into their territory.

★ **Think in the foreign language**. The skill of involvement can lead very quickly to this. In the early stages, you will inevitably pass through a period of translating in your mind from English into the language you're learning. This slows down communication. Though only the totally fluent bypass this process completely, it's possible to reduce it considerably by projecting yourself mentally (even visually and orally) into whatever situation or action is taking place, and playing the role of one of the partners in the dialogue. Many audio-based courses encourage this kind of projection and participation. It's a technique which may be described as 'entering into the spirit' of the language and its speakers.

14 How many words do I need to learn?

This question is a bit like asking, 'How long is a piece of string?' The answer depends on what you want to use the language for.

On holiday you can get by with 200 words. This is because situations which arise then are fairly predictable, and you can make a few words do a lot of hard work for you.

Most beginners' courses aim towards a target of 500–1000 words, which is a good start.

If you are more serious, the target to aim for is 2000 words. Where does this figure come from? In all languages, you find that some words are much more frequently used than others. Open your newspaper at a random page, and you'll find that 'the' occurs in almost every sentence. Other words aren't as frequent as this, but are still fairly common: for example, it's likely that 'said' or 'very' will appear on a newspaper page; but you wouldn't be surprised to find a whole page that didn't mention 'rheumatism' or 'beheading'. In English, 2000 words make up about 80 per cent of the language you see or hear in everyday life. That means that if you can recognise these 2000 words, you should be able to understand about four-fifths of the language you are likely to meet. Roughly the same figure applies to other languages.

Really serious learners won't be satisfied with understanding only 80 per cent of what they meet and, if you are one of them, you'll want to build up a bigger vocabulary. You'll have to work at it conscientiously. The most effective way of picking up a large vocabulary seems to be reading. You don't have to read novels or 'good books' to make this work for you. If you browse through a magazine filled with pictures you'll usually pick up lots of useful words. Children's books are also good, especially if you already know the stories.

Fluent non-native speakers of a language usually know at least 10 000 words.

15 Will I need to learn grammar?

This is rather like asking whether bricks and mortar, nuts and bolts are needed for holding your house together! Grammar is there whether we like it or not, whether we draw attention to it or not, whether we understand it or not. It's what holds language together.

Many adult learners have hang-ups about grammar, again partly because of the way they were taught French (or even Latin or English) at school. Either they are afraid of grammar and pretend it's not there, or they want lots of it when it's not really necessary! Some approaches encourage the learner to analyse grammar first, before getting into the language as a piece of communication. This can inhibit speech, and just doesn't appeal to everyone.

However, grammar, when presented at the right time and in the right way, can come in very handy. Its basic jargon (nouns, verbs, adjectives, etc.) provides the labels you need when you want to talk about how language works, which you sometimes have to do. In case you're baffled by some of the technical terms used in grammatical descriptions, we've provided a glossary (p. 180). We can save ourselves learning time by manipulating grammar – by understanding a small number of basic patterns and structures and transferring them from one situation to another. This ability, by the way, distinguishes the mere parroting encouraged by old-fashioned phrase books from a true learning course that teaches you how to use the language creatively.

So, will you need to learn grammar? The answer is: yes, you will, but there's no reason to get strung up about it!

16 Does my pronunciation matter?

Getting your pronunciation right is not always easy, but you shouldn't allow an imperfect pronunciation to stop you opening your mouth. On the other hand, if you make no effort to pronounce words the way the locals do, you can't be too upset if they don't understand you!

Getting the sounds right is important, but probably not as important as you think it is. It's much more important to sound fluent, even when you're not. You can do this by avoiding long pauses and hesitations, talking in short sentences rather than long ones, and, especially, by paying attention to intonation and stress.

Most good courses have a substantial and comprehensive audio component containing dialogues and exercises designed to help you get your pronunciation correct from the start, and you should make every effort to do so, by careful listening to, and careful imitation of, the models provided. It's much easier to cultivate a good pronunciation from the start than it is to correct bad pronunciation later on.

17 What's the best method for me to follow?

The simple answer to this is: the one that's best for you! There is no single, magic, painless, fastest, best way to learn a language. There are as many ways to learn as there are learners wanting to learn. So you must choose and develop the way that suits you. We hope that some of the suggestions made so far will help you do this.

There are many methods:

★ **Grammar-translation:** explicit grammar, and lots of translation into and out of the foreign language.

★ **Oral-aural:** lots of spoken language, extensive use of drills, not much reading or writing.

★ **Audio-visual:** not much stress on grammar, few drills, extensive use of pictures and tapes.

★ **Audio-lingual:** similar to oral-aural, but often including extensive use of language laboratories.

★ **Direct method:** all teaching takes place in the language you are learning, often on a one-to-one basis.

★ **Immersion courses:** compress a lot of learning into a

short time, usually several hours a day for a few weeks.

★ **Accelerated learning:** Suggestopaedia, Superlearning (p. 32).

These methods all have something to offer. But none of them should be thought of as *the* method!

★ **Feel free:** borrow and select from any or all of them; if it works, use it.

★ **Be varied:** use different materials and approaches to complement and supplement your main course book.

★ **Be flexible:** be prepared to accept that your target language works in apparently deep and mysterious ways, which are different from your own language. The French word '*pain*' means 'bread', but it's very different from what the word '*Brot*' means to a German, '*khleb*' to a Russian or, indeed, 'bread' to a Brit!

Make sure you choose a method that encourages you to do plenty of listening, and plenty of practising – and offers plenty of fun in the process!

So, what's the best method for you? The answer is: the one that you enjoy the most.

18 Will I find some languages harder than others?

There's no such thing as an intrinsically 'hard' language. Japanese is frequently described as 'the most difficult language in the world', but this doesn't mean very much. Certainly, the Japanese writing system (p. 87) is extremely complex, but you don't need to master it to speak basic Japanese; and spoken Japanese is no harder for English speakers to pronounce than, say, Italian. There are some aspects of Japanese grammar which are infinitely easier than many European languages, others which are quite unfamiliar – though they'd be more familiar to a Korean!

The relative difficulty of one language compared to another depends on two factors.

Language families

A language is easier for you to learn if it comes from the same language family as your own. If you're an English speaker, you'll find related European languages such as Dutch, German, Spanish or French easier than, say, Thai, Japanese or Korean. On the other hand, a Pole will find it easier to learn Russian or Czech than a French speaker will, since Polish too is a Slavic language.

Have a look at some of the language 'family trees' later in the book, and you'll see how these connections have come about historically. We've simplified them a little, in order to make the links between the main surviving languages more obvious.

Language features

Each language has a number of basic features the learner has to take into account: vocabulary, pronunciation and accent, grammar, alphabet, word order, idioms and so on. The relative difficulty of a language also depends on these features, irrespective of the language family.

Tone languages, for instance like Chinese (p. 122), Vietnamese or Thai are that much more difficult for Europeans to pronounce accurately than other Asian languages such as Japanese or Indonesian.

On the other hand, languages which are difficult in one respect can often be easy in another. The Japanese writing system is difficult for Europeans (and for most Japanese too!) but its pronunciation is straightforward. A Japanese has few difficulties reading Chinese, since the characters are virtually the same, but will have just as much trouble with the tonal system of pronunciation as a German would. French is not too difficult for English speakers to read, but it is difficult for them to pronounce – as generations of schoolchildren have discovered! A Russian will find it easy both to read and pronounce Greek, whereas an Italian will find Greek easy to speak but not so easy to read, and so on. Have a look at some of the 'Lingo' indexes that come later in the book. They'll give you a rough idea of what you'll find easy or difficult in various languages.

So, will you find some languages harder than others? It depends which skills you're talking about, and it depends which language you start from.

19 If I learn one language, does it help with learning others?

The short answer to this is: yes. The more languages you learn within a given language family, the easier it is to learn others within that family, or sub-group. So, for English speakers, once you've learned French it's that much easier to learn Italian or Spanish (although it's also easy to confuse them since there are so many similarities!); once you've learned German it's easier to learn another Germanic language such as Dutch; once you've learned Russian it helps with learning Serbo-Croat or Bulgarian, since these are also Slavic languages.

Learning any of the above won't necessarily, *per se*, help you to learn, for instance, Japanese or Chinese, since there are few natural connections to be made with these languages (apart from English loan words which they have borrowed in recent years).

What will help, though, is what we might call 'language-learning experience' or 'language sense'. Although riding a bicycle is very different from driving a car, you'll have gained a degree of 'road sense' in cycling which will help when you're learning to drive. If you learned to drive in a Ford Escort, driving a Cadillac or a Range Rover subsequently will feel different at first, but present few real difficulties in practice. And so it is with languages. Once you've been through the process of learning one language – grappled with its pronunciation, found out how to recognise and manipulate patterns and structures, learned how to build and guess at vocabulary, managed to spot both similarities and differences with your own language – the next one will be both easier and more enjoyable to learn.

You'll have gained a 'feel' for language-learning, developed a 'sense' of language. And that's when learning the next one becomes a lot of fun!

20 How do languages work?

All languages are different, but in some ways they are all very similar. It's a bit like people's faces. We all look very different, but we all share the same features: eyes, nose, mouth, and so on. The features that languages share are mainly to do with the way words are built up, and the order in which these words come in sentences. There are a small number of different ways of building words, and a small number of different ways of combining them into sentences, but many different languages can be made by combining these choices in different ways.

The main thing to look out for with a new language is the **word order:** the sequence of words in sentences. In English, for instance, we say:

John ate ripe bananas

In some languages, the equivalent words would come in different orders:

John ate bananas ripe
John ripe bananas ate
John bananas ripe ate
Ate John bananas ripe
Ate John ripe bananas

These basic word-order patterns also combine with a few other choices:

★ Some languages don't usually use *pronouns*, other languages always do.

★ Some languages don't have special words for 'a' and 'the'.

★ Some languages put the words for 'a' and 'the' after the noun they go with, instead of in front.

★ Some languages don't have special words for 'on', 'in', 'under', etc. They use special endings instead.

★ Some languages put the words for 'on', 'in', 'under', etc. after the noun they go with instead of in front of it.

You should be able to work out quickly which of these possibilities fit what your language does. Some language courses spend a lot of time giving you exercises that drill and practise these different word-order patterns. Try to work out a simple rule that explains what the exercise is all about, and then build your own exercises up using words that you already know.

The second thing to look out for with a new language is **the way words are built up.** In most European languages, words are made up of two parts called a *stem* and an *inflection*. The stem is the important part, which tells you basically what the word means. The inflections are the bits at the end which sometimes change depending on the job a word does in a sentence.

English doesn't have many inflections: lots of words don't change at all. In other languages, it's common for words to have many different endings, which can make it hard for English speakers to learn these languages.

The words that are most likely to change like this are nouns, adjectives and verbs. Here are some things to watch out for when you first start learning a new language.

★ *Nouns:* In most languages, nouns change their endings if they are plural. In some languages, they also change their endings depending on the job they do in a sentence. Watch out, too, for languages which have several different classes of nouns (*genders*). Genders sometimes affect other words in the same sentence.

★ *Adjectives:* Watch out for languages where adjectives have to change their form depending on the noun they describe. If this happens in your language, they are likely to be affected by the *number*, *gender* and *case* of the noun. (Check the glossary if these terms aren't familiar to you.)

★ *Verbs:* In most languages, verbs change their endings to show different times: a past action, a future action, an action that wasn't carried out, and so on. Watch out for languages that describe time in a way that's very different from English.

Watch out, too, for languages where the verbs are affected by the nouns in the sentence. In many languages, you will have to change the ending of a verb, depending on the main noun: whether it's singular or plural, definite or indefinite, and so on.

Some languages have special verb forms that can only be used for or by women.

Not all languages use inflections in this way. Some have changes at the beginnings of words as well as the ends. In others (Arabic and Hebrew are good examples), you will find changes in the middle of words, not just at the ends. In some languages, words don't change their shape at all; they stay the same, no matter how they are used.

Exceptions

As if complicated grammar wasn't already bad enough, all languages (except Esperanto) have exceptions and irregular words that don't behave like other words. There are usually good historical reasons for this, but that doesn't necessarily make them any easier to learn.

It will help if you remember that the most common words in any language are usually the most irregular ones that you will meet – most languages get more regular as you get to know them better.

English has lots of exceptions, but native speakers just

take them for granted. Foreigners learning English often spend a long time learning tables of verbs like:

give	gave	given
take	took	taken
sing	sang	sung
bring	brought	brought

Native speakers don't often worry about these forms – they are second nature to them. If you practise, the same thing will happen in the language you are learning. You'll get to use the exceptions correctly without thinking about them.

What kind of a language-learner are you?

This quiz helps you look at the way you think about yourself as a language-learner. Are you worried you won't succeed? Do you have the right attitude to get there in the end? Try this quiz and find out.

Tick one of the boxes alongside each of the statements, to show whether you agree or disagree with it.

SA = strongly agree
A = agree but not strongly
N = neither agree nor disagree
D = disagree
SD = strongly disagree

	SA	A	N	D	SD
1 I think I'm pretty useless at learning languages.	☐	☐	☐	☐	☐
2 You have to be much cleverer than I am to learn a language well.	☐	☐	☐	☐	☐

	SA	A	N	D	SD

3 I don't know why I'm bothering to try to learn a language. ☐ ☐ ☐ ☐ ☐

4 I wouldn't tell my friends that I'm learning a language. ☐ ☐ ☐ ☐ ☐

5 I don't think I'll ever be able to speak a language well. ☐ ☐ ☐ ☐ ☐

6 I don't really have time to learn a language properly. ☐ ☐ ☐ ☐ ☐

7 Learning a language certainly isn't much fun. ☐ ☐ ☐ ☐ ☐

8 People like me find it hard to learn languages. ☐ ☐ ☐ ☐ ☐

9 I don't see the point of trying to learn a language. ☐ ☐ ☐ ☐ ☐

10 Learning a language won't do me much good. ☐ ☐ ☐ ☐ ☐

11 Learning a language is more effort than it's worth. ☐ ☐ ☐ ☐ ☐

12 I wouldn't have a clue how to set about learning a language. ☐ ☐ ☐ ☐ ☐

How to score your answers

This quiz is all about self-image. The statements in the quiz are the sort that bad language-learners produce, so you score points for disagreeing with them.

Score:
5 points for each SD answer
4 points for each D answer
3 points for each N answer
2 points for each A answer
1 point for each SA answer

What your score means

More than 48 points

You obviously have a good self-image. You know why you're learning your language, and you know you can learn it. The effort doesn't frighten you, or put you off in any way.

24–47 points

You aren't completely convinced about this language-learning business, but you're willing to give it a go. Sometimes it doesn't seem worth it, but on the whole it does, and you think you'll get something out of it in the end. You probably think that the people you study with are much better than you, and you might worry that you'll never be able to speak really well.

0–23 points

If you scored less than 24 points, you might have a serious self-image problem. You aren't sure why you are bothering to put all this effort into learning a language, and you aren't sure that it will be worth it in the long run. More importantly, you aren't sure that you're really the kind of person who can learn a language. Oh dear! We hope this book will show you that even you can be a success at learning a language.

If you didn't score top marks in this quiz, you could benefit from a bit of positive thinking about learning a language.

Spend 2 minutes a day thinking about yourself: sit comfortably, close your eyes, and just imagine yourself in a situation where you are speaking fluent Arabic, or Russian, or Swahili, or whatever your language is. It's effortless, easy, fluent – and it's you doing it.

Think about how you'd like to be when you've learned your language. Will it change your life? Will it open new doors for you? Will you ever be the same again?

Give yourself a reward when you think you have achieved something. Perhaps you've got to the end of five chapters of your course book? Treat yourself! Make it a positive experience.

Feeling positive about learning a language is the best way to make sure you are a success.

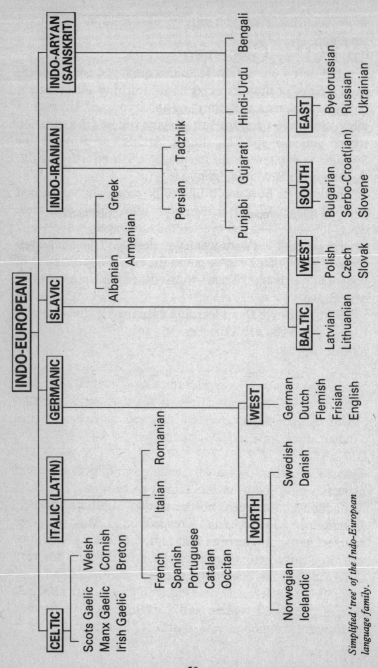

Simplified 'tree' of the Indo-European language family.

50

GO ON! German

Profile: Maureen Hart
Evening classes, Pronunciation, Listening

Germanic language family.

About German

> **German** is spoken by over 100 million people. It is the official language of united Germany, and Austria, and the main official language of Switzerland (where French, Italian and Romansch are also spoken).

German is spoken over a very wide geographical area, and dialects vary a lot from one region to another. The chief distinction is between northern and southern dialects (*Plattdeutsch* and *Hochdeutsch* respectively). Most language courses, national television and radio use *Hochdeutsch*, but you may come across varieties of German which are very different from this standard, especially in Switzerland.

There are German-speaking minorities in Holland, Belgium, Alsace-Lorraine and Luxembourg (where they also speak Luxembourgish – a dialect of German).

Since it is part of the same language family as English, German is a relatively straightforward language for English speakers to learn.

It is more or less phonetic (words are pronounced as they are spelt), its grammatical structure is more regular than that of most languages and pronunciation presents few major difficulties (especially if you are from Scotland, where the pure vowel sounds and guttural **ch**, as in lo**ch**, are akin to those in German).

As far as vocabulary is concerned, English speakers can easily recognise or guess at many German words of similar origin, and decipher or build other words once the basic principles of the language have been understood.

First, learn to spot the *cognate* words (p. 181). If you are on business in Germany you might find yourself staying at a *Privathotel* (private hotel, i.e. one that isn't part of a chain). All rooms (*Zimmer*) will be *mit Bad* (with bath) or *mit Dusche* ('douche' – shower) and, if you're lucky, there'll also be a *Schwimmbad* (swimming pool).

Second, get into the habit of breaking long words up into their component parts. German tends to make long words by adding short ones together to form compounds. To decipher their meaning you need good detective work and a few clues. It's often easier if you try starting from the end of the word.

For instance, if you're staying in a German hotel, there'll usually be a *Selbstwähltelefon* in the room:

telefon: cognate with 'telephone'
wählen: the verb to 'choose', 'select', 'dial'
selbst: cognate with 'self'

So, *Selbstwähltelefon* is a 'self-dial phone' – in other words, there's no need to go through the switchboard to make a call. Your hotel may also feature *Konferenzzimmer*, and, almost certainly, a *Hotelbar* where you can relax before dining out on the local *Spezialitäten*.

Guessing is very helpful when applied to German. See how

many of the following words you can recognise. Answers are
at the bottom of the page.

1 *Wein*   5 *Zentrum*
2 *weiss*   6 *Zentralheizung*
3 *grün*   7 *Schwung*
4 *schwimmen*   8 *kommen*

Clues: German frequently has 'sch-' where English has 's-';
'k-' for a hard 'c-'; 'z-' for a soft 'c-'. The ending '-ung' often
corresponds to '-ing' in English.

The word *Schwarzwaldschächtelchen* may seem daunting.
Broken down into its component parts, all is revealed:

schwarz: black
Wald: forest (compare English 'wood')
Schachtel: box
-chen: a common ending used to indicate a diminutive
        (something small or affectionate).

So, *ein Schwarzwaldschächtelchen* would be 'a little box
from the Black Forest'.
   And a *Streichholzschächtelchen* is a 'matchbox':
Streichholz: 'strike wood' – match.

Because of Germany's economic strength within Europe,
and in world markets, German has become increasingly
popular with vocational students and businessmen alike, and
'German for Business' or 'Business German' is now on every
self-respecting publisher's list.
   For additional advice on courses and materials for learning
German, try contacting the Goethe Institute (p. 176).

THE 'LINGO' INDEX FOR GERMAN

	Easy	Hard
Pronunciation	■■■□□□□□□□□□□□□	
Grammar	■■■■■■■■■■■■□□□	
Writing and spelling	■■■■□□□□□□□□□□□	
Vocabulary	■■■■□□□□□□□□□□□	
Reading	■■■■■■□□□□□□□□□	
Overall rating	■■■■■■■□□□□□□□□	

German pronunciation is fairly easy for English speakers. There aren't many unfamiliar sounds, and it helps that most English speakers have a good idea of what German ought to sound like.

The grammar is quite hard for English speakers: the main redeeming feature is that German is closely related to English, so you can usually find a parallel between what it does, and what English does. This will help you make sense of the complications and see the patterns more easily.

German has three genders, and a complicated system of cases. Adjectives and articles often change their form depending on the gender and the case of the noun that they go with. Verbs are also complicated, and there are lots of irregular forms. Word order is often different from English too – the most obvious features are that German often moves verbs to the end of a sentence, and often puts adverbs right at the front. Don't give up if you find German grammar daunting – it gets easier as you learn more.

German writing and spelling are relatively easy for English speakers. Some letters have accents, and there is one special letter ß (double 's') which might throw you at first, but you'll soon get used to it. Books published before 1945 were often written entirely in *Gothic script*, a form of the Roman alphabet that is initially very hard to read. It isn't normally used any more, though the letter 'ß' is still quite common, especially at the end of words. The vocabulary is fairly easy for English speakers. There are lots of cognate words, which make German easy for beginners to learn. More advanced vocabulary is a bit harder, but much of it consists of long words which can easily be broken down into their component parts.

German magazines and newspapers are generally on sale in most large towns in the United Kingdom, and you should be able to pick up television programmes in German if you have a satellite dish.

Maureen Hart

Maureen Hart is 53, and works as a secretary in a factory in South Yorkshire.

'When I started working here,' she says, 'we didn't have anything to do with overseas business, or export, but things have changed a lot in the last few years. I remember about 6 years ago, we had a phone call from a company in Germany. They didn't speak much English, and there was no one in the office who spoke enough German to take the call. I thought it was a bit daft, really, and I decided to do a course in German in the evenings.'

Maureen found her evening course pretty difficult. She didn't have a very good ear, and wasn't very good at picking up new words from listening, although she could manage fairly well if she was reading.

Maureen liked the social side of the classes she went to, but didn't actually learn as much from them as she had hoped. She worked better on her own with a textbook which contained lots of exercises. She found that she could usually get them right, though she had to spend a lot of time looking up words in the back of the book. The grammar wasn't any problem for her, but the vocabulary came only slowly, and she felt that she wasn't as good as some of the other people in the class.

After 2 years at evening classes, Maureen and her husband went on holiday to Germany. 'I had no trouble getting around in Germany,' she says. 'I knew most of the signs, and I could always understand what people said to me as long as they spoke slowly, and it wasn't too complicated. The trick was to ask people questions in a way that made them answer simply. For instance, you don't ask, "Where is the station?" because the answer you get is usually too complicated. So you learn to say something like: "The station. Left or right?"! I had a bit of trouble making myself understood, because my accent wasn't right, but I generally found that people were helpful if they thought you were making an effort.'

While she was on holiday, Maureen bought a lot of tapes of German pop songs, and when she got home to Britain she made a point of listening to them over and over, till she knew the songs off by heart.

Her main problems with learning German came in the area of pronunciation. The evening class that she joined had already been meeting for a few weeks, and she felt that the other students were much more advanced than she was. The teacher made a point of getting everyone to talk as much as possible, and Maureen felt that the other students were much better at this than she was. Everyone else seemed to be able to say things easily. Maureen found that she got stuck over words that were hard to pronounce, and this made her feel embarrassed and shy. She was just too conscious of her horrible accent, and so busy paying attention to the way she talked that she couldn't say more than a couple of words at a time without coming to a complete stop.

Fortunately, her teacher explained that almost everybody has this problem at the start, and showed her how she could make things easier for herself by speaking in short bursts rather than in long sentences. Long sentences are difficult to put together, and it's easy to get tongue-tied. It's much easier to sound convincing in a foreign language if you use short phrases.

Maureen had started to learn German just from a book. She didn't think of buying a course that also had a taped component. She'd read the pronunciation guide at the beginning of the book, but it wasn't really much help. It told her that the way German letters were pronounced wasn't always the same as in English, but she found it difficult to remember all the rules. Working on her own, with no one to correct her, she soon fell into bad habits. She almost always pronounced German words the way they would have been pronounced in English. When she started going to the class, she suddenly realised that she was on the wrong track, but didn't have a clue how to start getting things right.

Maureen's teacher showed her that there were some simple things she could do to improve her accent in German.

First of all, she showed her that thinking about the way the letters are pronounced was putting things the wrong way round. It was more natural to listen first, and think about the sounds. Then she could start thinking about the way the sounds she heard are written down. For instance, the German word for 'dog' is written *Hund*, and Maureen automatically pronounced the 'd' like a 'd' in English. It should have been more like an English 't'. She also pronounced the 'u' as she would have done in English. Left to herself, Maureen was saying something like 'harnd' when she should have been saying 'hoont'. In the end, Maureen found that

---

Deutsch, the German word for 'German', gives rise to the English word 'Dutch', which is used to describe the language and people of Holland, or the Netherlands. Dutch in turn gave rise to Afrikaans, the language of the Republic of South Africa.

when she learned words by reading them it was very hard to get away from the English sounds linked with the letters on the page. When she learned words by listening, this didn't happen quite so much.

Once she started to use her ears, she soon found that things started to sort themselves out. For instance, she noticed that you never get 'b' sounds, 'd' sounds or 'g' sounds at the end of German words, and soon realised that words spelled with one of these letters at the end are pronounced with a 'p' sound, a 't' sound or a 'k' sound. After that, it became much easier to pronounce words correctly.

Maureen still had some trouble with sounds that didn't seem familiar to her. The vowel sounds caused her a lot of bother. Although she worked in Yorkshire, Maureen had been brought up in London, and pronounced a word like 'no' something like 'nehoo'. Her teacher showed her how to use a small mirror to see the way her lips moved when she said 'no'. They started off slack and separated, and then moved close together into a tight bunch. Maureen learned that German vowels are much more like Yorkshire ones, where you don't move your lips. Once she learned to say 'oh', 'eh', 'ee' and 'oo' without moving her lips, she sounded much more convincing.

She had hoped that the pop songs she bought would help her pronunciation. She enjoyed singing, and after a few goes listening to the tapes, found that she could sing along with the music, especially if she kept the words in front of her. However, the songs weren't as much help with pronunciation as she'd hoped. She had to listen very carefully to hear what the voices were saying, and the words were often blocked out by the music anyway. As far as getting the sounds right went, the music didn't help her very much. However, she did find that she learned lots of new words and ready-made phrases, and it was easy for her to recognise these when she heard them in other contexts. Singing the songs in German made her feel much more confident about her accent, and stopped her getting stuck over difficult words. If she hesitated over a long word or a difficult sound, the tape just kept going and left her behind!

Maureen says, 'When we practised saying things aloud in class, it didn't really work for me. We couldn't practise a lot because the class was quite big. You only get a few goes on your own, and the teacher doesn't always like to tell you you aren't doing it right. So she says, "Good!" when you know that really it wasn't very good at all – but you don't know why it wasn't good. I found that singing the songs along with the tapes helped me to stop worrying about individual words, and that made me much more confident in class.'

She says: 'I still have trouble answering the phone in German, but the letters we get in the office don't bother me!'

What kind of a language-learner are you?

Maureen had a lot of trouble with the fact that German spelling isn't the same as English. The same letters are used in different ways. Is this a problem for you? Try this quiz and find out. Answers are given at the base of this page and the following page.

Question 1
Here are 10 English words spelled in an unfamiliar way. What are they?

1 duht	6 statyooet
2 fawm	7 tohst
3 satliet	8 fedhə
4 raydiayt	9 pahtrij
5 pəmishn	10 prayz

---

1 dirt 2 form 3 satellite 4 radiate 5 permission
6 statue 7 toast 8 feather 9 partridge 10 praise

Question 2

Here are 10 English words spelled properly. How would you
write them using the same system as in Question 1?

1 dirty   _____

2 formal   _____

3 total   _____

4 prose   _____

5 file   _____

6 fiction   _____

7 ice   _____

8 mail   _____

9 restore   _____

10 further   _____

How to score your answers

Question 1

Score 1 point for each word you got right.

Question 2

Score 2 points for each word you got exactly right. 0 points
for a near miss.

_____

7 ies 8 mayl 9 ristaw 10 fuhdha

1 duhti 2 fawml 3 tohtl 4 prohz 5 fél 6 fikshan

What your score means

Whatever language you are learning, you'll find that it has sounds which aren't the same as sounds in English. Like us, lots of languages use the Roman alphabet, but because they use different sounds, the link between them and the letters won't always be what you are used to. Some people, like Maureen, find this is a problem. If you start off learning your language from the printed page, your knowledge of English will interfere with your new language, and make it hard for you to learn to pronounce it properly. It's always best to start learning a language from a tape or from a combination of book and tape.

0–10 points

It's hard to convince some people that what they see written down isn't always what they hear. Perhaps you're one of them. Are you really sure that there's an 'l' sound in 'calm' and 'palm', and a 'd' sound in 'adjust' and 'adjacent'? You probably did quite well on the first question, but had difficulty with the second one. You have to learn to rely on your ears, instead of using your eyes all the time.

11–20 points

You made a few mistakes, but not very many. You might have a bit of trouble when you first start learning a new language, but once you've heard a lot of it, you aren't likely to be bothered by minor variations in the spelling system.

21–30 points

Well done! You soon realised that there was a system to the spellings we used here (they are pronunciation spellings taken from a dictionary). Not only that, you could use the examples we gave you in the first question to make a good guess at how to answer the second one. No language with Roman letters is going to be a problem for you.

Remember

★ You need to use your *ears* not your *eyes* if you want to develop a good accent.

★ The way words are spelled isn't always a good guide to the way they are spoken. Don't let what you know about English get in the way of your pronunciation.

★ Listening and reading at the same time will help you to learn how your language writes its sounds. Don't be fooled by the way words are spelled – listen to the sounds.

GO TO IT! French

Profile: Barry Smith
Flexibility, Improvising, Lateral thinking

Romance language family.

About French

> **French** is spoken by some 57 million people in France itself, and by some 220 million as an official language throughout the world, including the *départements et territoires d'outremer* (overseas territories, or *Dom Tom*). This French-speaking world is often known as *la francophonie*.

French is the official language of both France and Belgium (alongside Flemish, a variety of Dutch), and one of the official languages of Switzerland and Canada (Quebec, where the variety of French spoken is called *le québecois*).

It is also the official language in Haïti and the Ivory Coast, and is widely spoken in various other parts of Africa, including the Congo, Tunisia and Algeria.

Varieties of French are also spoken in places as far apart as Monaco, Jersey and Louisiana, as well as in the Caribbean islands of Martinique and Guadeloupe, the South Pacific island of Tahiti, and the Indian Ocean islands of Mauritius and Seychelles – where the national language is a pidgin form of French known as Creole.

Creole simplifies the pronunciation, spelling and grammar of standard French. *Bonjour* becomes *bonzour*. *S'il vous plaît* becomes *silvouple*.

On an aeroplane you'll see the following signs:
ZILE SOVTAZ I ANBA OU SYEZ
(*le gilet de sauvetage est sous le siège*)
(The lifejacket is under the seat)

PA ZET SIGARET
(*ne pas jeter de cigarettes*)
(Do not throw cigarettes)

Languages other than French are spoken within France: Breton in Brittany, Basque in the Basque country of southwest France, Provençal in the Midi, Corsican in Corsica, Occitan in the south and in Alsace a form of German.

For generations in the United Kingdom, the learning of a foreign language has been synonymous with the learning of French. Indeed, many people have been put off learning languages by their experience of learning it at school. This is partly because of the methodology used to teach French in the past. It relied heavily on an analytical rather than communicative approach, stressing grammar and translation, with apparently no other motive than to enable students to read or even translate the great literary works of Racine, Molière or Jean-Paul Sartre! It's also partly due to the nature of the French language itself which, for English speakers at least, is one of the most difficult European languages to pronounce, spell or write correctly – even though past teaching methods required all three!

French was for centuries the language of diplomacy and commerce. In more recent years, its international significance has been challenged and overtaken by that of English.

In the past, the French could mock the British for the number of French words adopted by the English language (particularly in the field of *haute cuisine*, and the kind of good living enjoyed by *bon viveurs* and *gourmets* alike). Recently, the language traffic has been in the other direction: the influence of international media, advertising, trade and pop music has resulted in the invasion of the French language by English (particularly American English). As a result the average Frenchman sets off after a hard week's work to enjoy *le weekend*, which he may spend practising *le footing*, wearing *un jogging*, watching *le foot* on television, quenching his thirst with *un long drink* and satisfying his hunger with *un steak*, *un hamburger* or some other *fast-food*. Meanwhile, his wife, if she's not at home washing her hair with *un shampooing*, may be out doing *le shopping*. Having parked her car in *le parking*, she may buy *un sweat*, *un pull* or *un T-shirt*.

This linguistic invasion has given rise to the phenomenon of *Franglais*, a mixture of French and English, much loved by schoolchildren (and not a few adults) in both countries, though frequently denounced by such staunch defenders of the purity of the French tongue as the Académie française.

Since French is the most commonly taught language in the United Kingdom, an abundance of courses and other materials is available. Try contacting the Institut Français (p. 176) for further information.

THE 'LINGO' INDEX FOR FRENCH

	Easy	Hard
Pronunciation	■■■■■■■■■■■■■■	□□
Grammar	■■■■■■■■■■■	□□□□□
Writing and spelling	■■■■■■■■■■■	□□□□□
Vocabulary	■■■■■■■■	□□□□□□□□
Reading	■■■■■	□□□□□□□□□□□
Overall rating	■■■■■■■■■■■	□□□□□

French pronunciation is difficult for English speakers. French makes extensive use of vowels which don't occur in English, and learning a good accent means learning to hold your mouth muscles in a way that is unnatural for English speakers.

The grammar is quite complicated for English speakers. French has two genders, and adjectives and articles will generally change their forms, depending on the nouns they are attached to. French verbs are also complicated. They come in three main types, all of which use different patterns of endings to show different tenses. Word order in French is fairly similar to that of English, but adjectives generally follow the nouns they describe.

French uses the Roman alphabet, but has an extensive system of accents to show variations in vowel sounds. Spelling was deliberately made difficult in the eighteenth century – it was considered dangerous for ordinary people to be able to read and write. There is currently an active movement for reform.

French vocabulary is largely based on Latin, so if you speak Spanish or Italian you will be able to recognise a large number of words. Ordinary everyday vocabulary has distanced itself from its Latin origins, which you can see more easily in rarer words. A lot of English vocabulary is directly derived from French – it's part of the legacy of the Norman Invasion.

French newspapers and magazines are on sale in most big towns in the United Kingdom, and you may be able to find French films at your local arts centre.

Barry Smith

Barry Smith is 38, and is married to Marie, who comes from Brussels. Marie speaks French; Barry learned it at school, but dropped it after a few years and never got very far with it.

Barry says that language wasn't a problem for them until

they had children. 'Marie speaks really good English, and we've always talked English to each other. People say that getting married was a good way of learning a new language, but Marie and I always found we had more interesting things to do together! Her parents spoke English too, so it wasn't much of a problem when we went to visit them, and, in any case, Europeans are used to English people who speak bad French!'

Things got more complicated when their first child was born. 'Marie just talked to Paul in French all the time, and because I spent a lot of time away from home on business, because of my work, Paul really grew up speaking French. It was a bit of a shock to me: Marie could understand what Paul was saying, but I couldn't. At first, I thought it was just because she was his mother.'

Barry decided he'd have to make more effort to talk French and borrowed a short course from the library. 'But it didn't help much,' he says, 'because it was mainly tourist French, and I was more interested in talking about changing Paul's nappies than changing traveller's cheques.' In the end, he asked Marie to write out some little cards with useful words and phrases on them, and when he spent time with Paul he'd do his best to use these words. 'They weren't the sort of words you find in textbooks, though. Do you know the French word for "safety pin"?'

While Paul was young, Barry found that it was comparatively easy to use his French. He found it hard to talk to Marie in French, though, mainly because they had always spoken English together, and he found it a bit unnatural to discuss important matters in a hestitant, stumbling kind of way. Marie thought it was important for them all to talk French together part of the time. They eventually decided that bath-time was a good idea, so Barry made a point of bathing Paul in French whenever he was home. Bath-time was fairly repetitive, and after watching Marie bathe Paul for a few weeks, Barry soon learned what to say and when to say it. Paul understood what he meant, even when it wasn't absolutely accurate. Barry soon found that he could handle the bath-time situation without any bother, though he still felt a bit embarrassed talking French when Marie was around. It took him a long time to realise that she was really pleased at the efforts he was making.

As Paul got older, Barry found that things were more complicated. Paul's French is obviously much better than his own, and although Paul usually talks French to his mother, he almost always talks English with his father. Barry says, 'The trouble is that you spend years learning the words for plastic ducks and cuddly toys, and just when you've got the hang of it, you find they're into girls and motorbikes instead!'

There aren't any good language books for parents. Almost all the courses you can buy or borrow, and most of the classes you can go to, are aimed either at tourists or business people. Both are involved in very different situations from Barry's. A parent needs to learn different words, and different ways of using them. Business people stay in hotels generally, not on camp-sites, for instance. And not many of them have to cope with negotiating medicine for a child with tonsilitis.

Looking after young children is a very special situation. For a start, you don't expect them to talk to you the way an adult would. Barry probably learned in school that *mon père* means 'my father' in French, but most children would say '*papa*'. Next, you don't use the same sort of language when you talk to a child as you would to your boss. A lot of talk with young children isn't passing on information or asking questions: it's more about encouraging and rewarding the child for doing what you want, stopping accidents and providing comfort as needed. Native speakers of a language seem to be able to come up with the right sort of language automatically – they were all children once and can usually dredge up nursery rhymes and children's songs from the bottom of their memories when they are needed.

Barry's mother-in-law solved some of these problems for him. She used her video-recorder to tape a whole set of children's programmes on Belgian television, and sent them to him as a Christmas present. Barry used to watch them with Paul at the weekends when he was home from work. 'At first I felt a bit of a twit watching programmes like this,' he says. 'The people I work with would come into the office and talk about the *Late Night Movie*, and I'd been watching the French version of *Sesame Street*. But actually, the programmes taught me a lot. The way you talk to babies and young children is very different from the way you talk to an adult – the words aren't all that different, but the way you ask for things and the way you get children to do the things you want are really very odd. I picked that up pretty quickly from watching the videos because the same things kept coming back again and again: lots of common expressions, numbers and counting, colours, and ways of being polite, when you say '*tu*', when you have to use *vous* instead, and so on.

'The one thing I regret is that I never got over my hang-up about talking French with Marie. You'd imagine it would be easy, but it isn't,' he says. 'When you live with people all the time, though, you soon get to know what they're talking about, even if you can't get every word. In fact, with Marie, I often know what she's going to say before she's said it, no matter what language she says it in!'

When Paul got older, Barry and Marie found a Saturday school for French-speaking children and Barry took Paul along. This gave him the opportunity to practise his French with the other parents.

Eventually, Barry discovered that one of the French-speaking fathers was a keen chess player and, while Paul was in the class with the other children, the two of them played chess together in a quiet corner. Barry found that playing chess was much like bath-time with Paul. As with bathing Paul, the same sorts of situations kept cropping up and, once he'd learned the basic words and what to say when he won or lost, it was pretty easy to produce the right word or phrase at the right time, and appear amazingly fluent. Barry never felt that he was on top of things, but as long as the situation was fairly straightforward he could usually guess what his friend was trying to say, even when he couldn't understand every word. What he replied didn't matter all that much – it was really only a part of the game.

The Saturday school had other spin-offs. Some of the families had a steady supply of French magazines and children's comics, and people swapped them and passed them on once they'd finished with them. Barry wasn't really interested in *Elle* and *Marie Claire*, but he picked up a lot of French just looking at the pictures and reading the captions. It was useful vocabulary, too: furniture, domestic appliances, clothes, food – words you don't find in textbooks but need all the time at home. The best reading matter Barry found was a mail-order catalogue: 600 pages of full-colour photographs of household objects, tools, gadgets, etc., all clearly labelled and described in great detail in very simple French. Barry soon got a reputation for knowing the French names for obscure pieces of hardware.

What kind of a language-learner are you?

Barry Smith wanted to learn French to talk to his son, but the courses he could find were aimed at business people or tourists. That meant he had to improvise, and build up his own learning materials from whatever was at hand.

What could you do with a French mail-order catalogue to help yourself learn French? Give yourself 2 minutes, and write down as many things as you can think of.

What could you use a clay flower pot for (apart from planting flowers in it)? Give yourself 2 minutes to think of as many uses as you can – they don't have to be ways of learning French, but if they are you score treble points.

How to score your answers

There are no right answers for this quiz, but you get points for being imaginative and interesting.

The question about the flower pot is designed to work out how flexible you are in the way you look at things. Rigid thinkers find it hard to think of it except as a pot for growing flowers in. Flexible thinkers can look at a flower pot and see it in different ways. Why not use it as a pot for baking bread? As a humane mousetrap? As a piggy bank? As a penholder? As a doorstop? As a bed-warmer? Why not put an aniseed ball in the bottom and use it as a plant-watering device? . . .

The more flexible you are, the more likely you are to be a good language-learner. Flexible thinkers can find ways of using very unpromising material and situations to help them learn. They are also good at using limited linguistic skills effectively. You won't find a flexible thinker speechless or stuck just because he or she has forgotten a word.

You can develop this kind of flexible, lateral thinking with practice. In fact, learning a language is one way of doing so. Most language-teaching concentrates on rules and patterns, but a lot of really creative use of language is about breaking these rules, and finding connections that aren't obvious to everyone. When you can make puns in the language you're learning, you are really getting somewhere.

What would a flexible thinker do with a mail-order catalogue? Here are some suggestions:

★ Cut the pictures out, and stick each of them on the front of a file card; cut the descriptions out, and put them on the back. Use the cards for learning the names of the pictures.
★ Choose a letter at random. Give yourself 2 minutes to find in the catalogue as many things as you can beginning with that letter.
★ Imagine you're going on an expedition to the North Pole. Make a list of 20 useful things you could take with you.
★ Open the catalogue at random, choose an object on that page, and find five words that describe it.
★ Cut out the descriptions and stick them on real objects in your house.
★ Cut out the pictures and the descriptions. Spread the lot out on a table, and try to match pictures with descriptions.
★ Choose three objects at random, and work out what sort of person would own them. Try to explain why in French.

Remember
★ Make the most of what you've got in your immediate environment. You can turn almost anything into a language-learning tool if you have enough imagination.
★ Learn the kind of language that's appropriate for your situation. Don't buy a course that's completely irrelevant to your real needs.
★ Predictable situations let you use your language effectively. Learn to spot and make the most of the ones you know that you can cope with.

TOUGH GOING? Spanish

Profile: John O'Donnell
Vocabulary, Memorising, Using multi-media

About Spanish

Spanish is spoken by an estimated 280 million people world-wide. It is the third most spoken language in the world (after Chinese and English). The number of native speakers of Spanish is growing fast, due mainly to Latin America's rapid population growth and increasing economic significance. Some estimates predict that by the year 2000 Spanish may be spoken by more people in the world than English.

Spanish is the official language of Spain, Mexico, Guatemala, Honduras, Nicaragua, Costa Rica, El Salvador, Panama, Cuba, Puerto Rico, Dominican Republic, Colombia, Venezuela, Ecuador, Peru, Chile, Argentina, Uruguay, Paraguay and Bolivia, but not of Brazil, where the official language is Portuguese. It is also spoken in many parts of the United States, notably California, Texas, Florida, New York and Chicago.

Because of the Latin element common to English and Romance languages, English speakers can easily recognise and acquire hundreds of Spanish words right from the start – though of course the pronunciation may be very different!

It's not difficult to guess the meaning of these words:

1 *la capital*	4 *la región*	7 *la botella*
2 *la fruta*	5 *el vino*	8 *la universidad*
3 *la catedral*	6 *un café*	

And with a little more effort you can work out the meaning of the following:

9	*el norte*	12	*el padre*	15	*el centro*
10	*el este*	13	*el aeropuerto*	16	*las vacaciones*
11	*la madre*	14	*la plaza*		

Answers are at the base of this page.

The official language of Spain is Castilian Spanish, *Castellano*. This is the standard spoken in the northern region (*comunidad autonoma*) of Castile (*Castilla*), in and around Madrid, the capital of Spain. Some say the purest accent is to be found in Valladolid.

As in the United Kingdom, you'll hear a variety of local accents in Spain, though these aren't usually a barrier to understanding. The accent of the south (in particular Andalucia) has certain distinctive features:

★ The 'th' sound as in c**erveza** (beer) becomes an 's'.
★ The 's' sound at the end of words is less strong, and may be missed out altogether, so *buenos días* sounds like *bueno día*.

Some features of this southern accent are also found in the Canary Islands and Latin America.

The influence of the Moors (Moslem Arabs who ruled in Spain from the eighth to the fifteenth century) is also particularly strong in Andalucia, and the Spanish language is full of Moorish-derived words like *alcázar* (castle) and *alcachofa* (artichoke). **Al-** at the beginning of a place name shows that it was once Moorish: **A**licante or **A**lmería, for example.

In addition to local dialects and accents, some areas of

Spain have their own separate language: Catalan in Cataluña, Valencia and the Balearic islands; Gallego in Galicia; and Basque (Euskara) in the Basque country. These languages, which were suppressed during the Franco regime, are now flourishing. Catalan even has its own multi-media television course: *Digui! Digui!*

The differences between the Spanish of Latin America and that of Spain are no more than those between different parts of the English-speaking world – the slight variations in pronunciation noted above, and differences in vocabulary due to environmental or historical influences. Mexican Spanish contains many words of Aztec origin, for instance, and in turn native words such as *tabaco*, *chile*, *tomate* and *chocolate* have entered English and other languages. Standard Spanish will get you by in any Spanish-speaking country.

Spanish is increasingly important in international business and trade, and an increasingly popular option for adult learners. There are many courses, phrase books and other materials to choose from, for both peninsular and Latin-American Spanish. The Spanish government has set up the Instituto Cervantes to promote language and culture, and further information may be obtained from this institute (p. 176).

THE 'LINGO' INDEX FOR **SPANISH**

	Easy														Hard
Pronunciation	■ ■ ■ ■ □ □ □ □ □ □ □ □ □ □ □ □
Grammar	■ ■ ■ ■ ■ □ □ □ □ □ □ □ □ □ □ □
Writing and spelling	■ ■ ■ □ □ □ □ □ □ □ □ □ □ □ □ □
Vocabulary	■ ■ ■ ■ ■ □ □ □ □ □ □ □ □ □ □ □
Reading	■ ■ ■ ■ ■ □ □ □ □ □ □ □ □ □ □ □
Overall rating	■ ■ ■ ■ □ □ □ □ □ □ □ □ □ □ □ □

Spanish is a fairly easy language for English speakers to learn, and, given the numbers of people who speak it throughout the world, it's surprising that it is not more widely used as an international lingua franca.

Spanish pronunciation is fairly easy for English speakers (especially for Scots, who won't have any problems with the rolled 'r' sounds or the 'j', which is pronounced like the -**ch** in lo**ch**). The main problem for most English speakers is that the vowel sounds of Spanish are different from English ones.

Spanish grammar is easier than French, and very much easier than German. Spanish has two genders, and the usual agreement rules for adjectives and articles. However, you can almost always tell the gender of a word by its ending. Verbs come in three main types, and are moderately complex. They change form depending on their subjects, and to indicate changes of mood and tense. Word order in Spanish is very close to that of English, though you'll find that it is a bit freer. For instance, verbs are often moved to the beginning of the sentence; in English, they generally come in the middle.

Spanish spelling is very simple, so straightforward that some types of dyslexia aren't possible in Spanish. The writing is almost perfectly regular (only Bs and Vs are likely to cause you problems – and they cause problems for native speakers too).

Spanish vocabulary is largely based on Latin, and a large proportion of Spanish words have an English cognate word. English speakers can therefore develop large passive vocabularies fairly quickly. You should be able to read reasonably difficult texts quite quickly, especially if you already know another Romance language. Spanish also has a sizeable number of words of Arabic origin, which may cause you some difficulties at first, and you might not be able to take advantage of the cognate vocabulary in Spanish if your English vocabulary isn't well developed.

John O'Donnell

John O'Donnell is 30, and works as personnel manager for a road transport company in the Midlands. John's firm does a lot of work in Spain, and he often found himself trying to sort out the problems that his drivers faced there.

'I'd learned French at school,' he says, 'but it was all pretty basic, and I'd never really studied a language seriously. The firm sent me to Barcelona for a week, so that I could get a better feel for the sorts of problems our drivers had, and what sorts of training we could organise for them.'

John didn't have time to join an evening class, but he bought a multi-media Spanish package, and worked through it on his own before he went to Barcelona. 'It was a pretty good pack. I watched the video programmes twice a week for about 3 months, and I used to listen to the cassette programmes in my car driving to work and back. After I'd listened to each cassette half a dozen times, I could remember a lot of the dialogues pretty well – I mean, I couldn't repeat them, but I didn't have any trouble understanding what the people were saying. It surprised me, really, because there was hardly any English on these tapes at all, and when I first heard them they sounded just like Double Dutch. The course didn't explain much about grammar, but there were lots of exercises, and you could work out for yourself the sort of thing it was trying to explain if you thought about it for a bit. The only thing I found really hard was remembering that Spanish verbs change their endings a lot.'

John was less successful when he actually got to Spain: 'The first thing I found was that people in Barcelona don't speak Spanish: they speak Catalan. They understand Spanish, and if I spoke to them in Spanish, they'd answer me back in Spanish, but then they'd switch back to Catalan. All the talk in the office was in Catalan – in fact they were quite aggressive about it, so I felt a bit left out. It got better when I went out with the lorry drivers, but I had a lot of difficulty coping with people talking with very thick accents. On the whole, though, the sorts of situations you find yourself in when you're driving a lorry are pretty predictable, and you can get by with a bit of imagination and initiative. The only real problem was when the lorry broke down, and then I was hopelessly lost.'

John eventually decided that his lorry drivers needed some elementary survival Spanish, and a few phrases in Catalan, just to impress the customers. He decided that more serious emergencies couldn't be dealt with except in English, and so he set up a 24-hour English-speaking telephone number that his drivers could call when they needed real help.

John's main strategy when he was learning Spanish before his visit to Barcelona was listening to cassettes as he drove to work. The pack he used wasn't specially written for business people, or for English speakers, so almost all the material was in Spanish with not very much English. John found that it helped if he worked to a rhythm. Every Sunday night, he watched a half-hour video programme, which showed two people doing something together: having a meal, booking a room, getting their car fixed, and so on. Then over the next 5 days, he'd listen to the cassette tape that went with the video programme on his way to and from work. The cassette tapes contained a dialogue that was similar to the one on the video, and exercises that played around with the sentences in the basic dialogue. John says, 'At first I was really depressed by these tapes. Most of the exercises were what they call "Listen and Repeat" exercises. The voice on the tape says something, and you have to repeat it back. Sometimes, you have to repeat it back using a different word, and sometimes you have to change what you hear into something completely different. At first, I just couldn't get the hang of it at all. The voice on the tape would say something and expect me to repeat it – and all I could produce was one word or something like that. I thought I was really stupid, and almost gave up.'

Then, one day when John was walking home from the pub, not thinking about anything in particular, he suddenly noticed that Spanish phrases were floating through his mind. He wondered if he was trying too hard with his tapes, and expecting to do too much at one go. He decided that he'd stop doing the exercises out loud while he was driving. Instead, he'd just let the tape play and see how much he took in if he didn't make a big effort.

Surprisingly, this relaxed approach worked much better. By the end of each week, he'd listened to his cassette 10 times, and although he still couldn't produce the answers to order, he knew the tape pretty much off by heart. He certainly didn't have any problems understanding the sentences, even when they were just part of an exercise. And he knew what the right answer ought to sound like, even though he couldn't always produce it himself.

After 8 weeks, John had got through eight lessons of his course, and was beginning to feel that he hadn't made much progress. Then, by mistake, he took the wrong cassette with him to work – an earlier lesson that he'd found really hard. What surprised him was that he didn't find the exercises at all difficult now. He'd somehow got the hang of them just by listening to more advanced ones. After this, he started using Fridays to go over earlier tapes as a kind of revision.

John says: 'I'd read a report in *Which?* magazine that was pretty critical about the course I'd chosen to use. They said it was old-fashioned and didn't use the latest communicative methodology. But it really worked for me. Spanish is quite an easy language in some ways, but the way the verbs work is really hard: you have to remember to change the ending, depending on whether there is one person doing something, or more than one. And you have to change the ending depending on whether what you are talking about is taking place now or in the past, or in the future. It's pretty complicated. The tapes with the exercise drills went over all the variations again and again and again. In the end, by just listening to the tapes, I found that I'd picked it all up without really trying. It would have been a lot harder without the

> It takes longer to learn isolated languages which have no 'family connections'. Basque, spoken by over one million people in the French and Spanish Pyrenees, is completely unrelated to any other language.

video cassettes, though. I'm not sure I would have worked out what was going on if I'd only had the audio tape and a book.'

John also made a special effort to learn the vocabulary used in the exercises. At first, he tried to avoid learning the words because he thought he'd just be able to pick them up by listening. He actually found that listening was much easier when he'd made an effort to learn the words first.

He worked out that each lesson in his course contained something like 100 new words. He thought that was a lot, but breaking his learning schedule down into 20 words a night made it easier. A friend who had been a soldier told him that the army reckons you can learn 60 words a night if you are on a language course. John tried this, but found he couldn't keep it up for more than a few days. Even 20 words was tough going. He couldn't learn them in less than half an hour and, even then, often found that he forgot five or six of them immediately afterwards. Of course, the fact that he was bound to come across them next day on the tape helped a lot. He'd usually remember what a word meant when he met it in the context of a story or a dialogue, even when he couldn't remember what it meant on its own. By the time he'd listened to the tape twice a day for 5 days, there weren't many words that caused him problems.

'What worked for me,' says John, 'was listening to the cassettes lots of times. Some courses give you the impression that if you just listen to a tape once, or watch a video once, you can learn a language just like that. I couldn't even pick up three phrases doing it that way. Listening to the tapes over and over again was a bit like being hypnotised. I don't suppose that I learned very much from listening once, but the second time, I learned a new little bit, and remembered the first little bit. And the third time, I learned another little bit, and remembered the first two little bits, and so on. Lots of little bits soon mount up to something pretty substantial. I was really surprised how much I could say when I went to Barcelona.'

What kind of a language-learner are you?

John found that he couldn't learn long sets of words off by heart, but he might have been able to do better than he did if he had used a memory system. This doesn't work for everybody: it depends whether you are a visual person or a verbal person, and how tolerant you are. If you think you are intolerant, don't even consider trying the method we've outlined below. If you are a visual thinker, you'll find the method very easy. If you are a more verbal thinker, you'll need to adapt it a bit.

Try this test, and see how good you are at visualising. First, read this extract from a thriller. Then, cover up the story, and answer the five questions below, without looking back at what you read. The questions will ask you about details that the story *doesn't* provide. You have to say how clearly you can see them in your mind.

'The killer moved stealthily towards the bed where his victim lay asleep. Was it always so easy to kill somebody? The dagger rose and fell, glinting in the moonlight. On the bed, a sudden movement, and a slow red patch spreading on the sheet.'

Tough going?

	Very clear	**Hazy**	**Very unclear**
What was the killer wearing? How clear is your image of this?	☐	☐	☐
Which side of the bed was the killer standing on?	☐	☐	☐
What colour hair did the victim have?	☐	☐	☐
Where was the window relative to the bed?	☐	☐	☐
Where was the victim stabbed?	☐	☐	☐

How to score your answers
There are no right answers, of course.

Score:
2 points for every 'very clear' answer
1 point for every 'hazy' answer
0 points for every 'very unclear' answer

The higher your score, the more of a visual thinker you are, and the easier you'll find it to use memory techniques to learn vocabulary.

Making connections

When you learn a word in a foreign language, you learn two things. The first is what the word means; the second is the way it looks or sounds. (You also need to learn how it's used, but we'll forget that for the moment.) Most textbooks concentrate on teaching you to learn what foreign words mean. Unfortunately, just learning what words mean is only a small part of learning vocabulary. The much bigger part, for most learners, is making a connection between the sound or shape of a word and its meaning. The meanings are easy; what's hard is remembering which word fits with which meaning.

Memory methods (sometimes called *mnemonics* from the Greek word for 'memory') help you learn foreign words by making them harder to forget. If you learn a list of 20 words using ordinary methods, you'd expect to have forgotten half of them by the next day. If you use a memory system, you should be able to remember them for much longer. Some people can learn 100 words in an hour like this. Maybe it will work for you. It's worth giving it a try, anyway.

One mnemonic method that works for some people is called the *keyword* method. It's based on an age-old technique of associating pictures or images with the words you want to learn. Here's how it works.

You want to learn the Spanish word *ducha*, meaning 'shower'. First you find an English word that *ducha* reminds you of, one that sounds like *ducha*, or one that looks like *ducha*. 'Duchess' would do. 'Duchess' is the keyword for *ducha*. This gives you:

Spanish word	Keyword	English word
ducha	duchess	shower

Now, think up a picture which involves both the keyword and the English word. It helps if what you conjure up is funny, amusing, obscene or memorable in some other way. The more bizarre it is, the more you are likely to remember it. For *ducha*, you might think of a duchess in a shower – make sure that she is wearing a tiara and lots of jewels, otherwise you won't remember that she is a duchess.

Once you've constructed your picture, close your eyes for 10 seconds, and think about it. That's all there is to it.

Most people's reaction to this suggestion is: 'How stupid!' However, there's no doubt that the system really does work for some people. What seems to happen is that the image focuses your attention on the shape of the word you are trying to remember, and this keeps it in your memory a bit longer than usual. You'd imagine that thinking up the image and keeping it in mind would actually make it harder for you, and clutter up your brain. But it doesn't. After a while the images just fade away, and you are left with a direct connection between *ducha* and 'shower'.

If your score in the visualisation test was low, this method might not work for you. You're perhaps more verbal than visual, and you may find that you can use verbal connections instead. For instance, for you, just saying '*ducha*, the duchess, shower' four or five times might be better than trying to think up a picture. Or you might be able to construct a crossword clue for yourself: Sounds like making tea in the shower (5 letters). The important thing is to decide what works for you, and then use it.

Also derived from Latin . . .

Italian is spoken by over 60 million people. It is the national language of Italy, and one of the official languages of Switzerland. It is also spoken by a large number of immigrants throughout the world in 'Little Italy' communities, for example, in the United States, South America, Australia and the United Kingdom. It has also been the first foreign language of parts of North Africa such as Somalia, Ethiopia and Libya.

Italian is perhaps the closest of all the Romance languages to the parent language, Latin. Since more than half of all English vocabulary derives from Latin, Italian is therefore one of the easiest European languages for English speakers to learn. It is also, to the English ear at least, one of the most beautiful. Italian words have lots of vowels and relatively fewer consonants than English words. This makes Italian a very easy language to sing. A large number of ordinary

Italian words have been borrowed into English in connection with music: *adagio*, *allegro*, *andante*, *arpeggio*, *cadenza*, *coda*, *concerto*, *da capo*, *forte*, *opera*, *pianissimo*, *sonata*, *tremolo*, *vibrato*, *vivace* – to name but a few.

Romanian, also descended from Latin, is the official language of Romania, and spoken too in parts of Yugoslavia, Hungary and Bulgaria. The Moldavian language of the Soviet Socialist Republic of Moldavia is Romanian written in Cyrillic script.

Portuguese is closely related to Italian (and even more to Spanish). It is the national language of both Portugal and Brazil and is spoken by over 10 million people in the former and over 130 million in the latter. Portugal initiated the age of discovery – *as descubertas* – and colonisation, and was one of the last nations to abandon its colonial empire. As a result, Portuguese is still spoken also in the Azores and Madeira; in Goa in India; in Angola, Mozambique, Guinea-Bissau, Sao Tomé and Principe and Cape Verde in Africa; and in Macao, Indonesia and Timor in Asia. This means that world-wide there are over 160 million speakers of Portuguese.

Remember

★ You won't be able to do the exercises on a tape first time through. Courses often imply that you can, but they are frequently being unrealistic.

★ You can learn a lot just by listening to tapes over and over again while doing something else. This kind of incidental learning is more powerful than you'd expect.

★ Visual images can help you learn vocabulary. They don't help you learn the words much faster, but they do make it much harder for you to forget what you've learned.

GOING OFF THE IDEA?
Japanese

Profile: Frank Mack
Writing systems, Speaking and reading, Comic strips

About Japanese

> **Japanese** is spoken by some 124 million people, confined to the islands of Japan: Honshu, Hokkaido, Kyushu and Shikoku.
>
> A dialect of Japanese (almost a distinct language) is spoken in the Ryukyu Islands, including Okinawa.
>
> Japanese is also spoken by substantial Japanese communities on the west coast of the United States and Canada, in Hawaii and in South America (mainly Brazil).

The precise origins of Japanese are a subject of much controversy. There are those (usually Japanese) who claim it has no known connection with any other language in the world. Others admit that it is relatively isolated, though they observe some grammatical similarity with the Altaic group of languages which includes Korean, Mongolian and Turkish. Even here, however, the vocabulary is completely different.

What seems clear is that there is no direct connection between Japanese and Chinese as languages, though the influence of Chinese upon Japanese is enormous. From about the seventh century, the Japanese imported from China, then the greatest civilisation in the world, a wide range of cultural phenomena including Buddhism, Confucianism and the Chinese writing system. Japan at that time did not have one of its own, and so adapted the Chinese writing system to represent its own spoken language.

Inevitably, there were grammatical features of Japanese which could not be conveyed by the Chinese characters (or *kanji*, meaning 'letters of the Han dynasty', as they became known) and the Japanese soon adapted some *kanji* for use as two sets of symbols (representing syllables) to express these features: *hiragana* and *katakana*. The latter is now mainly used to convey the sounds of foreign loan words brought into the language.

This complex writing system, consisting of Chinese characters, or *kanji*, on the one hand, and the two syllabaries *hiragana* and *katakana* on the other, together with the language's relative isolation from other languages, has contributed towards the reputation of Japanese as being 'the most difficult language in the world'. Indeed, when foreign missionaries first came to Japan in the sixteenth century the language was dubbed 'the devil's tongue' because of this complexity. After the Second World War the Americans, the occupying power in Japan, wanted to abolish the writing system, on the grounds that it was a serious obstacle to education and development. They failed.

Certainly, to read and write Japanese is a formidable (though not insuperable) task. However, it is perfectly possible to learn to speak the language without getting involved with the writing system. When Japan opened up to the outside world in the nineteenth century, after more than two centuries of complete isolation, a romanised writing system was developed by foreigners for foreigners to learn to speak Japanese. It is a system, slightly modified, which still exists today, although most Japanese, though they learn it at school, find it hard to read.

You need some 2000 characters to be considered literate in Japan, though you can get by with about 900.

★★	the two characters for Japan : *Nippon*, or *Nihon*, the land of the rising sun
★★★	*Nihonjin*: Japan person, or Japanese
★★★	*Nihongo*: 'Japan language', or the Japanese language
★★★ ★★	*Nihonjin desu*: I am (he/she is/we/you/ they are) Japanese

Japanese is both flexible and adaptable: in recent years, many foreign loan words (especially English ones) have been borrowed by Japanese, but transformed in such a way as to be almost unrecognisable.

Many such foreign words are contracted or abbreviated:

wāpuro is short for *wādo purosessā*: word processor
pāsokon is short for *pāsonaru konpyūta*: personal computer
wanpiisu: one-piece suit
sando: short for *sandoitchi*, e.g. *hamu sando*: ham sandwich

English is not the only language to be absorbed in this way: *arubaito* is from the German word *Arbeit* (work), but is used to refer specifically to the kind of part-time work undertaken by students. The French word *avec* (with) has become *abekku*, and has come to mean a young couple (someone 'with' someone else). Many Japanese 'love hotels' are called *Avec* – or even, nonsensically to English speakers: *With*!

There are more opportunities now to learn Japanese than ever before. For advice, contact the Japan Information Centre, Embassy of Japan, or the Japanese Language Association (p. 176).

THE 'LINGO' INDEX FOR JAPANESE

	Easy → Hard
Pronunciation	■■■■□□□□□□□□□□□□
Grammar	■■■■■■■■■■□□□□□□
Writing and spelling	■■■■■■■■■■■■■■■■
Vocabulary	■■■■■■■■■■■□□□□□
Reading	■■■■■■■■■■■■■■■■
Overall rating	■■■■■■■■■■■■■□□□

Japanese is traditionally considered to be a hard language to learn, mainly because of the difficulties of the writing system. This aside, a number of features of Japanese actually make it easier to learn than many European languages.

Japanese pronunciation is fairly easy for English speakers. There are a couple of sounds in Japanese that don't occur in English, but they will not cause you any serious bother.

Japanese grammar is simple, compared with that of many European languages. The main difference is that verbs come at the end of sentences in Japanese, so that the structure of sentences is completely different from English. To compensate for this, there are no genders, no articles, no distinction between singular and plural nouns and, though verbs change their form to indicate tense, these changes are regular and predictable.

Japanese does have a complicated system of respect language, which is tied up with the niceties of Japanese social etiquette and the subtleties of cultural behaviour. It requires special attention on the part of the learner.

Japanese writing is extremely difficult. It's possible to learn to speak without knowing how to read, but if you are a serious learner of Japanese you'll have to tackle the writing system sooner or later.

Although Japanese has borrowed lots of words from English, most of the vocabulary is not related to English, or to any other language you might know. This means that Japanese is a hard language to get started in, but the more words you know, the easier it gets to pick up new ones.

Frank Mack

Frank Mack lives on Tyneside, and works in a Japanese electronics factory. He's 47. The company offered classes in elementary Japanese as part of its extensive social programme, and Frank decided to take part, even though he'd never learned a language before. 'They gave us the chance of learning French at school,' he says, 'but generally the boys thought it was a sissy language, and we did something else instead.'

Frank was surprised to find that he was quite good at learning Japanese. 'We had a class every Friday afternoon at four. A Japanese lady came and taught us simple phrases, and how to be polite. It was dead easy: in fact, the most difficult thing about it was watching my boss having a really hard time of it.'

After a few weeks of the elementary class, Frank felt that he wanted to take this a bit more seriously. The teacher offered to teach some of the class how to read and write Japanese – until then they'd been using Roman letters, but the teacher said that if they wanted to make any serious progress they really needed to learn to read and write in Japanese. Frank thought he had always been good at drawing, and decided to give it a go.

'It was a lot harder than I was expecting,' he says. 'In English, you just have 26 letters and once you've learned them you can read and write anything – well almost anything. In Japanese it's different. You have to learn hundreds of characters, and you can't even use a dictionary if you don't understand how the system works. You need to be very precise when you are writing Japanese: every character needs to be just so, with the strokes all made in the correct order. At first, I found it really frustrating, but the teacher gave us some simple books, the kind of books that children use in Japan when they are learning to write. We simply copied the characters, and learned to read simple stories that we had written out.'

Frank found that he could learn the characters fairly easily as long as he practised them a lot. The teacher told the class that they would need about 900 characters to be able to read Japanese, and made them learn 15 characters a week. Copying them out was a great help. Frank found that he couldn't always remember what a character meant, but after a while, if he looked at a Japanese newspaper he could recognise the characters he had been learning. His teacher used to provide the class with old newspapers, and Frank took to circling all the characters he thought he knew with a red felt-tip pen. At first he only recognised a few, but after a few weeks, the number of red circles on each newspaper article was impressively high. Frank still couldn't understand the articles, but at least he could see he was making progress.

Frank says, 'Some of my friends said you could learn Japanese without bothering about the writing. I suppose they might be right, but the writing added a new dimension to it all for me.'

Learning a language with a new writing system is a lot harder than learning one that uses Roman letters. If you are working on your own, you may find that the course book you use starts off by teaching the new writing system. It will show you all the letters or characters, ask you to learn them and then, after a few lessons, will carry on as if you could read them all perfectly. This isn't really a good idea. It's bad enough learning to do things in a new language when you aren't too sure of the words. When you have to struggle to learn to read the words as well, the psychological load is too much for most people.

Frank's teacher obviously realised this. She started off by teaching the class to speak Japanese phrases, especially greetings and phrases to do with politeness. Then, when the class already knew some words, she showed them how to write them down. The general rule is learn to read and write words that you already know and recognise.

This is especially important in Japanese because of the way the writing system works. In European languages, the letters stand for individual sounds – even in English, where the spelling system is really complicated, there is usually some connection between the letters you write and the way the word sounds. In most European languages, the connection is very simple and straightforward. In Japanese, it's more complicated. Frank's teacher explained that Japanese children usually learn to read using a syllabic writing system, where you have one written sign for each syllable. So the sound 'ka' is written in one way, but the sound 'ko' is written in another. They don't look at all similar.

Unfortunately, as Frank discovered, Japanese writing for adults is even more complicated; it uses a writing system borrowed from China, as well as the simpler syllabic one. Frank found it hard at first – even when he used simple books with huge print the characters all looked the same. Also, he couldn't see any connection between the way words were written and the way they were pronounced. His teacher said there was a connection of sorts, but it couldn't easily be explained to beginners. That was a great help!

Frank found that learning 15 characters a week was more than he could cope with. He forgot them much too easily.

After a couple of months, his teacher brought a set of comic books to the class. Frank was surprised, because he'd always thought of them as being for people who were a bit thick. The teacher explained that in Japan it was quite common to read comic books – even economics textbooks are sometimes written in comic format!

Frank took home a couple of Kung Fu comics, and tried to

work his way through them. They were written in adult writing, with both characters and *kana* syllables, so they were quite difficult to understand. Frank couldn't read the writing very well, but it was pretty easy to work out what the story was about, just by looking at the pictures.

The teacher said there weren't all that many words in these comics, and produced a small dictionary for each one of them. Frank found that he could use this to help him get through the comic.

Many of the words were greetings and simple social phrases, and seeing them in the comics helped Frank see how they are used – in Japanese, you have to be careful to use the right level of politeness and formality, depending on who you are talking to.

The pictures also helped. Sometimes he'd come across a word he didn't know, but its meaning would be obvious from the picture.

At first, Frank noticed that he could get through about a page of his comic in half an hour. After a while, though, he found that the same words kept coming back again and again. He knew that because he put a little tick in the dictionary every time he looked a word up. He was surprised how many of them he ticked more than once.

When he'd finished the comic, his teacher told him to read it again. Frank was disappointed at this: he'd been expecting to go on to another one. He soon realised, though, that he was able to read his comic much faster the second time. By now, he knew exactly what the story was, and only looked words up in his dictionary when he wanted to check that he was right, or if he'd forgotten how a word was pronounced. The third time he read the comic, he hardly needed to look up any words. It was obvious he was making real progress.

Frank says: 'I would never have thought of using comic strips to learn a language, but it really did help. You read them over and over again. It's a bit like an actor learning lines for a play. The best thing was when I managed to use something that I'd read in the comic in the class – it just came out naturally at the time I needed it.'

What kind of a language-learner are you?

Because English is so important in the modern world, many languages have taken English words into their vocabularies. When this happens, the words often change their shape so that they look more like ordinary words in the language they've been borrowed by.

In English, lots of words have clusters of consonant sounds – two or three consonants in a row. In Japanese, this doesn't happen very often: consonant sounds are usually separated by vowels. So when Japanese borrows English words with consonant clusters, it usually adds vowels between the consonants to make them sound more Japanese.

In English, we have lots of words that end in a consonant. Japanese words almost always end in a vowel. When Japanese borrows a word that ends in a consonant, it usually adds a vowel to make the word feel more Japanese.

Japanese doesn't use all the sounds that English does. 'L' and 'r' aren't separate sounds in Japanese as they are in English. English words with an 'l' sound often end up with 'r' sounds in Japanese. Japanese doesn't have a 'z' sound; it uses 'j' instead. And it doesn't have a 'v' sound; it uses 'b' instead.

On the next page there is a set of English words that Japanese has borrowed and changed to look more like natural Japanese words. How many of them can you recognise? You'll find it helps if you say the words aloud several times. The answers are at the base of the page. Try *all* the Japanese words before you look at the answers.

1	*appuru pai*	16	*gorufu*
2	*anaunsā*	17	*hanbāgu*
3	*basukettobōru*	18	*handobaggu*
4	*bēsubōru*	19	*hankachi*
5	*bijinesuman*	20	*herikoputā*
6	*biiru*	21	*hoteru*
7	*direkutā*	22	*hotto doggu*
8	*doru*	23	*intabyū*
9	*esukarētā*	24	*jānarisuto*
10	*Furansu*	25	*jerii*
11	*firumu*	26	*karifurawā*
12	*furiiza*	27	*magajin*
13	*furūtsu jūsu*	28	*kontakuto renzu*
14	*futtobōru*	29	*māmarēdo*
15	*garēji*	30	*painappuru*

How to score your answers
Score:
2 points for every word you got right.
1 point for every try, even if it was wrong.

What your score means
If you scored really badly (well under 25) on this test, you may be the kind of learner who has difficulty developing a good accent in a foreign language. Some people find it hard to separate the way a word is written from the way it sounds, which makes it difficult for them to get used to the idea that

---

1 apple pie 2 announcer 3 basketball 4 baseball 5 businessman 6 beer 7 director 8 dollar 9 escalator 10 France 11 film 12 freezer 13 fruit juice 14 football 15 garage 16 golf 17 hamburger 18 handbag 19 handkerchief 20 helicopter 21 hotel 22 hot dog 23 interview 24 journalist 25 jelly 26 cauliflower 27 magazine 28 contact lens 29 marmalade 30 pineapple

letters don't always have the same values in different languages. You may have scored badly because you were scared to guess. Guessing is always a good strategy in learning a language. You might be wrong, but you'll soon find out if you are. If you don't even try, you never get anywhere.

If you scored well (over 40) on this test, you may be the kind of learner who is good at finding a way past the writing to the sounds they represent. That probably also means you are good at developing a foreign accent.

On the other hand, it may be that you are simply the kind of learner who enjoys puzzling things out, and that you aren't put off by superficial differences in the way languages are written down. You might have managed to solve these puzzles by reversing the changes Japanese made to the English words – chopping off the final vowels, changing the 'r's to 'l's and so on, and getting rid of the vowels in the middle of words – and seeing what you were left with. If this is how you did it, you need to find a way of using your ears more, and relying less on conscious rules.

Remember

★ If you have to learn a new writing system, it helps to learn to speak the language a bit first. It's always easier to read a word you know than a word you don't know.

★ Learning to read is easier if you learn to write at the same time. Practising the writing will help to fix the forms of the characters in your mind, and make it easier for you to recognise them when you see them.

★ Books with pictures are easier than books with words. Don't be snobbish about what you read in your foreign language: comic strips and kids' books may teach you more than literary classics.

HAVE A GO! Welsh

Profile: Jim Saeed
Intensive courses, Grammar, Having a go

```
                   ┌─────────┐
                   │ CELTIC  │
                   └─────────┘
          ┌────────────┴────────────┐
     Scots Gaelic              Welsh
     Manx Gaelic              Cornish
     Irish Gaelic             Breton
```

Celtic language family.

About Welsh

> **Welsh** is now spoken only in Wales, and in a small Welsh-speaking community in Patagonia (Argentina). About half a million of the three-million-strong population of Wales claim to be Welsh speakers. Though the overall proportion of people speaking Welsh has declined to about 20 per cent, some areas are 80 per cent Welsh speaking.

There has been a spectacular growth of interest in bilingual education in Wales, and many more young people now speak the language. Children can choose to do the whole of their education in Welsh if they wish, and many do. There is a Welsh language television service (S4C) and radio service (Radio Cymru). Among adults, there is a good deal of interest in learning Welsh, particularly on residential and intensive courses (WLPANs). For further information, contact Canolfan Iaith (p. 177).

Scots Gaelic

Historically, Gaelic was mainly spoken in the Highlands and Islands, where economic decline and depopulation led to the decline of the language.

Since the mid-1960s, however, a major revival has taken place in Scottish consciousness, and with it increased support for the Gaelic language in education, broadcasting, publishing, commerce and the arts.

Gaelic continues to be spoken as a community language throughout the Western Isles, in parts of Skye and in some of the islands of Argyll. The largest community of Gaelic speakers is now to be found in Glasgow.

Irish

Irish is the indigenous language of Ireland, though after several centuries of anglicisation, it is now spoken as a native language by only a small minority (1 per cent or 2 per cent) of the population, mainly in the west of Ireland. Nevertheless, in the Constitution of the Republic of Ireland, it is recognised as the first official language, and is widely learned at school. Though not an official working language of the European Community, it has 'treaty' status.

Cornish, Manx, Breton

★ The last Cornish speakers died in the eighteenth century.
★ The last Manx speakers died in the 1940s.
★ Breton is still spoken by about half a million people in Brittany in France.

THE 'LINGO' INDEX FOR WELSH

	Easy	Hard
Pronunciation	■■■□□□□□□□□□□□□	
Grammar	■■■■■■■□□□□□□□□	
Writing and spelling	■■■□□□□□□□□□□□□	
Vocabulary	■■■■■■■□□□□□□□	
Reading	■■■■■■■■■■□□□□	
Overall rating	■■■■■■■■■■□□□□	

Welsh has a reputation for being a hard language to learn, but it's probably not as difficult as people generally think it is. There's currently a great deal of support for learners of Welsh and, unlike many languages, you don't have to travel a long way to find a place where it's spoken.

Welsh pronunciation is pretty easy for English speakers, with the one exception of the 'll' sound, which doesn't appear in English.

The grammar is tricky for English speakers. The verb is usually right at the beginning of a Welsh sentence, so sentences are structured very differently from English ones. Adjectives come after the nouns they describe. Welsh has two genders, and adjectives sometimes change their forms depending on the gender of the noun they go with. Verbs vary greatly according to their subjects, and to indicate different tenses. Unusually, prepositions also vary if they accompany a pronoun.

A particularly difficult characteristic of all the Celtic languages is that they have a system of 'mutations' – changes to the consonant at the beginning of a word. This makes it difficult to look words up in a dictionary until you understand the system.

Welsh spelling is very straightforward once you realise

that 'y' and 'w' are vowels. It is more or less phonetic.

Welsh vocabulary contains a lot of English loan words, and many that are basically Latin in origin. The changes in sound from Latin to modern Welsh are extensive, though, and most English speakers would be hard put to recognise Latin words, even if they also spoke another Romance language.

The vocabulary becomes easier the more advanced you are: infrequent words are often made from more frequently used ones that you are likely to know.

Jim Saeed

Jim Saeed lives in Cardiff. He's 25 and an actor, but he spends a lot of time between jobs. Jim decided that he might as well do something useful when he wasn't working, so he signed on for a course in Welsh. The university runs special intensive courses, five mornings a week, for 10 weeks, specially aimed at adult beginners.

Jim says, 'I'm not Welsh, my Dad came from Somalia, and my Mum was from Jamaica, but I've lived here all my life, and I thought I'd give it a go. I speak a bit of Arabic, and I've got a bit of school French, so I thought I'd find Welsh pretty easy, maybe even get a job on Welsh television. A Welsh-speaking black actor: there must be lot of jobs for people like that . . . .!'

Jim is a born mimic, and can imitate other people's accents very easily, and very accurately, so he had no trouble with the pronunciation. 'I'd lived in Cardiff, and it was easy to pick up the way Welsh sentences go up and down. The sounds were a bit difficult at first, especially the

---

The longest place name in the world:

LLANFAIRPWLLGWYNGYLLGOGERYCHWYRNDROBWLLLLANTYSILIOGOGOGOCH

known locally as LLANFAIR PG.

"ll" thing, but I asked the teacher to help me get it right, and after that I didn't have any problem. I was used to learning lines, too, so I didn't have any trouble learning vocabulary. I used to take a list of about 20 words, and put them into a little story, mostly in English, but with Welsh words here and there. Then I'd write the story down on a file card, and learn it just like I'd learn any other part. Twenty words a day for 10 weeks is quite a lot of words.'

Jim says that he found Welsh hard in other ways. 'Putting the verb at the beginning of a sentence instead of in the middle struck me as a bit peculiar, and I was surprised to find that lots of languages work like that. I was really puzzled over why Welsh words have so many different forms. I mean, you get used to English words changing their endings – Arabic and French do that too – but why would you want to change the beginning of words like you do in Welsh?'

Jim found that he liked the intensive course a lot. 'It was pretty difficult getting up early in the morning, but it was a lot better doing it every day than it would have been once a week. You could feel yourself getting better fast.'

He says that the only thing he didn't like about the class was the way it insisted on you getting things right all the time, and the way the teachers corrected even tiny mistakes. 'I wasn't really bothered if I got things wrong a bit. I knew that people would understand me, and if I got really stuck I knew that I could always switch into English. But I was glad that I didn't really have to do that very often. I'm pretty fluent now. My main problem is that when I go into a pub in west Wales and ask for a pint, people always answer me in English. I guess they just can't cope with a black Welsh-speaker!'

Jim went on an intensive language course, rather than on a course that only met once a week. He felt that the main advantage was that it didn't give you a chance to forget anything you'd learned. It was fairly exhausting, but he could see that he was making progress, getting better by the day.

Minority languages are increasingly receiving official support. The European Bureau for Lesser Used Languages in Dublin lists the following lesser used languages. They include majority languages used by small communities in neighbouring states:

Arbrësh	Français	Kernewek
Catalá	Euskara	Franco provençal
Hrvatski	Brezhoneg	Cymraeg
Furlan	Lingua corsa	Lallans
Griko	Dansk	Aromaneasca
Ladin	Deutsch	Balgarsca
Occitan	Frysk	Turkce bileyorum
Sardu	Nederlands	Polski
Slovensko	Gaeilge	Letzeburgesh
Gallego	Gaidhlig	Frasch
		Seeltersk

You can obtain information about these languages from the bureau (see p. 177).

He measured his progress by the number of times he got stuck for a word – pretty often at first, but less and less so as the course went on. 'It wasn't so much that I'd learned a huge vocabulary,' he says, 'but the teacher taught us ways of using what we did know to get round problems. By the end of the 10-week intensive course, I wasn't really fluent, but I didn't often get really stuck.'

It was an advantage learning a language in an area where he could use it almost straight away. He says: 'Some of the children who live in my street go to a Welsh school, and they always talk Welsh. It was fun learning things in the class in the morning, and then being able to try them out immediately on the kids in the afternoon.'

Jim was also able to make use of television and radio broadcasts. If he'd been learning Dutch or Italian, he'd have needed a satellite dish to get television programmes, but learning Welsh, he could just use an ordinary television set. 'I found the best thing to watch was soap operas,' he says. 'They broadcast the best ones with English subtitles on teletext, so you can listen to the Welsh, but read the English at the same time. At first, it was just fun to see how much I could recognise. When I first started the course, I couldn't get much more than "hello, please, thank you and goodbye," but there's quite a lot of that in soap operas, so you feel as though you are making progress quickly. After a couple of weeks, I'd learned a lot of words, and I was beginning to recognise some of them on the television. It was much easier to recognise the words if I had the subtitles on. If I turned them off, it suddenly all went back to Double Dutch, and I couldn't recognise a thing.'

Soap operas also showed Jim all sorts of different ways of using the language he'd learned in class. 'In class, the teacher taught us things like asking for directions, buying things in shops and ordering drinks in a pub, but it was sort of artificial. When I watched people doing these things on television, it seemed more real. And if you have a pub scene with five people buying drinks, they don't all use the same words, so you learn different ways of saying things, almost without trying. What I really liked about the soap operas was that they showed you people doing ordinary things that you knew you'd want to do yourself.'

Jim had a lot of trouble with formal grammar while he was learning Welsh. Although he'd done a bit of French at school, it had been taught orally, and he'd never learned some of the technical terms that other people in the class seemed to use with ease. At first, he felt really stupid when he had to ask what nouns or adjectives were, but he soon discovered that he wasn't the only person who didn't know.

The teacher explained that you don't need to know this technical terminology to talk a language – young children learning English manage to speak it pretty well without knowing what an adverb is. The only real advantage of the technical terms is that they sometimes help to explain in a simple way how Welsh is different from English.

At first, Jim was anxious to get things absolutely right. He noticed that the teachers almost always corrected the students when they got things wrong, and made them say things over and over until they were right. He always tried to avoid mistakes, and kicked himself whenever he said anything that turned out to be wrong. 'When you're an actor, you get so used to doing everything spot-on that you think mistakes are really serious, and you do your best to get things perfect.'

One of his teachers explained that making mistakes is actually a natural part of learning a language – a bit like the way children say 'I goed' and 'I wented' instead of 'I went'. Mistakes like that don't matter all that much. Teachers will usually correct them, but that's because you have to be corrected if you're going to get them right in the end. In real life most native speakers will be able to work out what you should have said, and will understand your meaning. They may think what you said was funny, but they'll still understand you. Vocabulary mistakes are much more important than grammar – if you ask for a beer in grammatically perfect Welsh when you really want an orange juice, no one will realise that you've made a mistake, and you won't get what you really wanted.

The teacher also explained that even native speakers aren't always sure of the grammar of their language. Languages are always changing, and the grammars change just like the sounds and the vocabularies. In English, for instance, many people now say 'If I was you . . .' whereas not so long ago 'If I were you . . .' was the proper thing to say. Most languages have grey areas like this. One of the difficulties about Welsh is that words often change their beginnings, and learners spend a lot of time getting the hang of these 'mutations'. In fact, native speakers often also get them wrong.

'Once I stopped worrying about grammar, and learned to concentrate on getting my message across,' Jim says, 'it was much easier!'

What kind of a language-learner are you?

Some learners are naturally good at finding patterns in the way languages work. Once they get the hang of it, they find it easy to use with different words, and in different ways.

The test below is designed to see if you can spot patterns in a language you don't know. It is not Welsh; it's a language we've made up to illustrate some points about grammar. Read the sentences carefully, and try to work out which bits mean what.

ek kum chuchu	The train is coming
ek namas chuchu	The train is very big
nek kum niva chuchu	The train isn't coming
ek chuchu	It's a train
ek moris	It's a car
ek flup trakibas	There isn't any room in the bus
ek tichi moris	The car is very small
ek bast trakibas	The bus has broken down
nek niva bast moris	The car hasn't broken down
nek niva flup trakibas	There's lots of room in the bus
ek bast trakibas akid	Has the bus broken down?
ek stop chuchu	The train has stopped
nek stop niva chuchu	The train hasn't stopped

How would you translate these sentences?

1 It's a bus
2 The bus is very small
3 The train is full
4 The car has broken down
5 Is the train coming?
6 Isn't the bus full?
7 The car is very big
8 Has the car stopped?
9 Isn't the car coming?
10 Is the bus full?

Answers are at the bottom of the opposite page.

Now make up five other sentences with the words you know.

_____

_____

_____

_____

_____

How to score your answers

Score:
5 points for each sentence you got completely correct.
2 points for every sentence you got nearly right.

Give yourself 5 extra points for each of your own sentences, whether they are right or wrong – you don't get anywhere if you aren't willing to have a go. With the words we've given you, there are more than 200 sentences that you could have made up.

10 ek fiup trakibas akid
8 ek stop moris akid   9 nek kum niva moris akid
6 nek niva fiup trakibas akid   7 ek namas moris
4 ek bast moris   5 ek kum chuchu akid
1 ek trakibas   2 ek tichi trakibas   3 ek fiup chuchu

What your score means

0–15 points
You seem to have a lot of trouble working out the differences
between languages. And that's not all: the differences annoy
you and make you cross. You probably wish that all
languages were the same or that, if they have to use different
words, they could at least use them in the same way. You
might have scored badly because you can see the patterns,
but find it hard to describe what you see.

Have a look at the section 'How do languages work?'
(p. 43) and see if it helps you.

16–30 points
You don't find this part of learning a language easy but at the
same time, it doesn't really put you off. You find it a bit of a
nuisance that other languages aren't quite like English, and
you sometimes find that the explanations in books aren't
much help.

Have a look at our section 'How do languages work?'; it
explains some of the more curious aspects of language, and
will show you what to look out for in a new one.

30–51 points
This is a pretty good score. You are obviously picking up
some of the patterns, but sometimes jump to the wrong con-
clusions. Have a look at the patterns we've listed below: they
are almost all to do with what goes where in a sentence. Are
you looking for something more complicated, perhaps? Or
did our translations confuse you?

51–75 points
You certainly don't have any problems in this department.
The fact that a language is different from English doesn't
bother you in the least, and you have no problem in using a
few words in many different ways. You've also realised that

you don't get points for being a blushing violet where learning a language is concerned. It's always worth having a go.

The patterns you should have noticed were:

★ Ordinary sentences begin with *ek*.
★ What the sentence is about (the subject) usually comes at the end of the sentence.
★ Questions are formed by adding *akid* to the end of an ordinary sentence.
★ Negative sentences always contain *nek* and *niva*.
★ *Bast*, *flup*, *tichi* and *namas* always come after *niva*.
★ *Stop* and *kum* always come between *nek* and *niva*.

Remember

★ If you can find the time and money, intensive courses are better than once-a-week ones. They don't give you a chance to forget what you are learning, and quickly get you to the stage where you can become an independent, self-supporting learner.
★ Films and videos with subtitles are an easy way of picking up new vocabulary.
★ Don't worry about getting the grammar absolutely right. It's more important to sound convincing than to be absolutely correct. Most native speakers make allowances for the odd mistake.

KEEP GOING! Russian

Profile: Brenda Johnson
Using video, Overload and revision, Measuring progress

Slavic language family.

About Russian

Russian is a member of the Slavic branch of the Indo-European language family. This branch is in turn connected to the Baltic language group, which includes Lithuanian and Latvian. Neighbouring Estonian is part of the Finno-Ugrian group of languages (p. 172).

Russian is the official language of more than 270 million people in the Soviet Union (USSR). Each republic also has its own national language: from Uzbek and Tadzhik in Central Asia to Georgian, Armenian and Azerbaidzhani in the Caucasus. In other parts of the USSR (which covers one-sixth of the world's land mass) there are literally hundreds of dialects.

The Russian alphabet

The Russian alphabet is called Cyrillic after the missionary St Cyril, who is thought by some to have devised it in the ninth century. There are 33 letters including the 'hard' and soft' signs.

А	Б	В	Г	Д	Е	Ё	Ж	З	И	Й	К	Л	М	Н	О	П	Р
a	b	v	g	d	ye	yo	zh	z	i	i	k	l	m	n	o	p	r

С	Т	У	Ф	Х	Ц	Ч	Ш	Щ	Ъ	Ы	Ь	Э	Ю	Я
s	t	u	f	kh	ts	ch	sh	shch	–	y	–	e	yu	ya

★ Some letters **К**, **О**, **М**, **Е**, **Т**, **А** look and sound very much like their English (Latin) counterparts.

★ Some letters look like Latin letters, but have different sounds (e.g. **С** = 's'; **Р** = 'r'; **Н** = 'n'; **В** = 'v').

★ Many Russian letters are derived from the Greek, and yet others are derived from Hebrew.

★ Sometimes a single Russian letter constitutes a word: **И**, meaning 'and'.

Using these clues, and the key above, you should be able easily to decipher these two well-known abbreviations:

    1 ТАСС   2 СССР

You should also be able to make out the following common words in regular use in everyday Russian:

1 оркéстр	3 винó	5 пáпа	7 таксú	9 ресторáн
2 парк	4 мáма	6 метрó	8 пианúст	10 теáтр

Answers are at the base of the page.

Finally, with careful detective work, and bearing in mind that a single Russian letter sometimes requires several English letters, see how many of these famous Russians you can recognise. See below for answers.

1 ЧЕХОВ	4 ЧАЙКОВСКИЙ
2 СТАЛИН	5 ГОРБАЧЁВ
3 ЛЕНИН	6 ПУШКИН

It should by now be obvious that the Russian alphabet is not nearly such a huge obstacle to learning the language as might at first seem. It will not take you as long as you might think. Once you have mastered it, the way to the language itself will also be clear and you will see that, in spite of daunting Latin-like inflections, case endings and so on, Russian is, as the writer Anthony Burgess wrote, '. . . as rich and satisfying as Christmas pudding.'

Though it may be some time before your Russian is up to reading Pushkin in the original, learning enough to get by on a visit to the Soviet Union, whether for business or pleasure, is no more difficult for English speakers than either French or German.

There is no shortage of course materials, and the Russian Teachers Association and the Great Britain-USSR Association (p. 176) can offer information to anyone wishing to start learning Russian.

Of the other languages in the Slavic group, Serbo-Croat(ian) is useful if you're travelling in most parts of Yugoslavia (Slovene is spoken in the north). With the democratisation of Eastern Europe, Polish, Czech and Slovak will soon become more accessible and useful languages for travel and business.

---

1 Chekhov   2 Stalin (actually a Georgian!)   3 Lenin
4 Tchaikovsky   5 Gorbachev   6 Pushkin

THE 'LINGO' INDEX FOR **RUSSIAN**

	Easy	Hard
Pronunciation	■■■■■■■■■■■□□□□□	
Grammar	■■■■■■■■■■■■□□□	
Writing and spelling	■■■■■■■■■■□□□□□	
Vocabulary	■■■■■■■■■□□□□□□□	
Reading	■■■■■■■■■■□□□□□	
Overall rating	■■■■■■■■■■□□□□□	

Russian pronunciation is moderately difficult for English speakers. There are a few unusual sounds which don't occur in English. The real problem is that the syllables making up the words tend to be more complicated than we are used to in English, with combinations of consonants that our language doesn't allow. There are also 'soft' sounds and 'hard' sounds which are difficult to imitate accurately – though you'll still be understood if you get them wrong.

The grammar is complex. Nouns come in three genders, and each of them has a complicated system of case endings. Adjectives change their form depending on the gender of the noun they describe, and its number and its case. Verbs, too, have a complex set of ending changes to show different aspects of time. The way Russian handles time is different from the way English does.

Russian writing is less difficult than it looks. Spelling is very regular, and once you understand which letters go with which sounds, you should not find it a problem.

Russian vocabulary is often related to words that you might know in other European languages. A lot of the harder vocabulary is made up of elements that you will quickly become familiar with in the basic vocabulary.

Brenda Johnson

Brenda Johnson is a local government officer. She's 30. The city where she works is twinned with Voroshilovgrad in the Soviet Union and from time to time the two cities organise a programme of exchanges and visits. The last time a visit was arranged, Brenda was part of the organising team, and thought it would be a good idea to learn a bit of Russian in time for the visitors' arrival in the United Kingdom.

'I'd always wanted to learn Russian,' she says. 'They used to teach it in the school I went to. I was going to do Russian for O-level, but they abolished it before I got the chance, and we had to do French instead. This visit from the people in Voroshilovgrad was just the excuse I needed.'

Brenda and her friend borrowed a video-tape course from her local library, and they decided to work through it together – they thought they could practise when they got home from work. They also thought they'd be less likely to give up when the going got tough if they were both learning the language at the same time.

At first, they decided to watch the tapes on Sunday afternoons, and to do the homework on their own whenever they could. That worked for a couple of weeks, but it was one thing to watch a video on a wet Sunday afternoon in February, and something quite different on a fine day in spring. That routine soon started to slip and, in any case, Brenda found that watching the video once wasn't really enough. Eventually, they settled into watching the video programme three times a week over tea after work. 'To be honest,' says Brenda, 'it wasn't as good as *Neighbours*, but we were used to watching television after work, so it wasn't really a change of routine for us, and it didn't interfere with going out in the evening. The best thing about the tea-time routine was that while I was washing up, things that I'd heard or seen on the programme would go round and round in my head. I noticed that happening even on days when I hadn't watched the video tape. It was as though my brain was learning Russian even when I wasn't conscious of it.'

Brenda nearly gave up after 4 weeks: the excitement of learning a new language was beginning to wear thin. She felt that the course was really going too fast for her – too many new words, and too much new grammar all at once. Her friend was finding it hard going too, but they worked out that they must be learning something, because the first lessons were really easy when they went back to them.

Brenda says: 'It was all worth it when the Russians came. We weren't exactly fluent, but every time we spoke in Russian, they all cheered. My boss was so impressed that we're on the team for next year's return visit to Voroshilovgrad.'

If you are teaching yourself a language using a course book, you have to look out for the problem of overload. Most textbooks take it for granted that you will learn anything they try to teach you. In real life, no one manages to learn everything at one go. After a few lessons, the gap between what you actually know and what the course book expects you to know, gets too big to handle. This can cause problems for unconfident learners. There are two main areas where this kind of overload happens. The first area is vocabulary, and the second is grammar.

The problem with vocabulary is that some course books introduce new words faster than you can learn them. The first lessons usually aren't too difficult, because they use a limited vocabulary and everything is explained. After four or five lessons, though, most people have forgotten about half the words they learned in the first ones.

The problem with grammar is that textbooks often teach you grammatical patterns, but don't help you to get on top of them – you know the pattern, but you don't use it automatically, without thinking about it.

These two problems together are a recipe for disaster. Exercises that you would find really easy in English are very hard if you don't know the words, and if you have to think all the time about the grammar. As long as you are working with a limited vocabulary, and simple rules, learning a language is easy enough. But most learners get very depressed when they get into overload, and lots of them give up altogether.

For Brenda, this bad patch arrived after 5 or 6 weeks of her Russian course. The course material suddenly seemed to get very hard. Her first reaction was to blame herself. She knew that she hadn't done very well at languages in school, and thought that she must be the kind of person who couldn't learn them at all. 'I really felt like giving it up,' she says. 'It was just so hard. The course book made it look as though the exercises ought to be really easy, but it was taking me half an hour to do an exercise that only had a few lines in it. Honestly, I had to look up every word sometimes, and by the time I'd found out which word I wanted, I'd forgotten what I wanted it for. And if I had to look up five or six words in a sentence, I couldn't keep them all in my head at the same time. It was *so* tiring, and it made me feel *so* stupid.'

Fortunately, Brenda's friend was more experienced at learning languages than she was. She showed Brenda that a lot of the trouble she had wasn't her fault; it was just that the course was going too fast for her. They eventually decided that they needed to go more slowly, with lots of revision. Brenda's friend worked out a three-steps-forwards-and-two-steps-backwards system. They still stuck to one lesson a week, but when they had done three whole lessons, they'd drop back two, and start again.

Brenda found that organised revision made her feel much better about the way she was learning Russian. The exercises were always much easier the second and third times round. She noticed especially that things she had really struggled with the first time were often very simple the second time.

But she still felt that she wasn't making a lot of progress, and thought it would have been a good idea if the textbook had included some simple tests that could have showed her that she was getting better. 'When I used to go to keep-fit classes,' she says, 'they had charts where you ticked off what you could do, and you could tell you were getting better because your score kept on going up. Why don't they have things like that for languages?'

The simplest way of measuring your progress in a foreign language is to find out how quickly you can find words in the language you are learning. It's only a rough measure of your progress: knowing words isn't everything, but generally speaking, the more fluent you are with words, the better you will be with other things as well.

Here's how the self-test works. You need a watch with a second-hand, a pencil, a piece of paper and a pocket calculator.

Think of an English word and write it down. Now think of another one that's connected to it in some way, and write that down. Now think of another word that's connected to your second word, and write that down. Keep going for 2 minutes. It doesn't matter what you write down, as long as there is some sort of connection between the words. You'll probably manage about 15 or 20 words in 2 minutes.

Now do the same in your foreign language.

You'll find that the number of words you write down in your foreign language is a lot less than you wrote down in English – the foreign words aren't as easy to find, and the connections aren't as easy to make as they are in English, so each connection takes longer.

You score this test by dividing your foreign score by your English score, and multiplying the result by 100. For example, Brenda got 20 English words in 2 minutes, and 10 Russian words, so her score is 10 divided by 20 multiplied by 100 = 50.

The higher your score, the more fluent your vocabulary is becoming.

Brenda did this test once a week, and kept the results on a chart on the wall. 'It wasn't as impressive as press-ups,' she says, 'but at least I could see I was making progress, even when I felt I wasn't getting anywhere.'

What kind of a language-learner are you?

Good language-learners are able to make a little language go a long way, and do a lot of work for them. This test is designed to work out how resourceful you are with language.

1 Describe an egg, but don't use any words that contain 'e'.

2 Here's a list of five words taken at random from a dictionary. Put all of them into an English sentence. You'll need to add some extra words, but the fewer extra ones you need, the more points you get. You can change the words by adding endings if you wish.

NEXT   NICE   NIGHT   NOISE   NOSE

3 Rewrite this sentence as simply as you can:

'Provided that you have proof of purchase, and that your apparatus has not been subjected to misuse or accidental damage which is excluded from this warranty, any defect in this apparatus which appears within 1 year of the purchase date will be made good, subject only to a nominal charge covering reasonable transportation costs where such charge is deemed to be appropriate.'

How to score your answers

There are no correct answers for this test. The simplest way to score what you've written is to get a friend to do it for you.

1 Show your friend your definition, and ask him or her to tell you what you are describing. Give yourself 10 points if they guess correctly, five for a near miss.

'E' is the commonest letter in English, so asking you to use words which don't contain 'e' stops you from using English in the way you normally would. It's not really like using a foreign language, but it forces you to find different ways of saying things. Good language-learners usually find this task easy. You didn't have to use a whole sentence for your description, of course. Something like 'a thing for holding a yolk' might do, or even 'ostrich big, sparrow small, round thing'. It partly depends on who your description is for. A good language-learner would take this into account.

2 Score 10 points if you used fewer than five extra words; five points if you used five or more extra words; no points if you didn't try. Ask your friend to decide whether your effort makes sense or not. Our effort was: 'Next night, his nose produced nicer noises.'

Good language-learners are clever at using few words to great effect.

3 Ask your friend to score your simplified version for you. You score points for using short sentences, and simple vocabulary, and you lose points for using jargon words like 'deemed'. Give yourself 10 points if your friend thinks your version is really simple, five for fairly simple, and no points if he or she can't understand it. Our version was: 'If this apparatus breaks down within a year, we'll fix it for you. You'll need to show us your receipt. There's no charge for repairs, but we might have to charge you a transportation cost. If you've treated your apparatus badly, or if it's been damaged in an accident, we will not mend it for free.'

Many people think that complicated ideas can't be expressed in simple language. They are more impressed by complexity than by clarity. They use very long sentences, and use technical words where they aren't really necessary. Good language-learners use language in a simple and concise way. If you try to say something long and complicated in a foreign language, you will always run into serious problems. If you do get stuck, though, there is usually a simpler way of putting what you are trying to say.

The higher your score, the more likely it is that you will be the kind of learner who can use little bits of a foreign language effectively.

Remember

★ Learning a language is more fun if you do it with a friend. You can practise with each other, and help each other over the rough patches.

★ Don't give up if you think you aren't making progress. Even if you feel completely stuck in one area, you're probably making a lot of progress in others.

★ Keeping a progress chart will help your motivation. Try to make your progress more obvious by proving to yourself that things are easier, or faster, now than a month ago.

GO FOR IT! Chinese

Profile: Ann Nelson
'Get by in . . .' courses, Trying it out, The real thing

About Chinese

Chinese is the most spoken language in the world, with almost 1000 million native speakers. Over 70 per cent of the population speak 'Mandarin' (a term used in the West, but not by the Chinese themselves), or *pŭtōnghuà* – 'common speech'.

Mandarin Chinese is the most widely used form of the language, the one promoted by the Chinese government as the national language of China, a kind of lingua franca. It is also used in Taiwan.

Mandarin is based on the Beijing (Peking) dialect, and is the form of Chinese most visitors to China will come across when dealing with shops, hotels, restaurants, banks and so on all over the country. In many rural areas, regional dialects still predominate, however.

Some 50 million people speak Cantonese, the dialect used in Canton, Hong Kong, Guangdong province and Singapore. If you want to chat to the waiter in your local Chinese restaurant he's more likely to speak Cantonese than Mandarin.

Chinese characters have traditionally been a unifying factor, enabling all Chinese, from whatever province, speaking whatever dialect, to communicate with each other at least in writing.

Chinese writing is completely unlike the alphabets we use

in the West. Alphabetical writing systems represent the individual sounds that make up a word. Chinese writing represents sounds, and meaning, in a less direct way. The earliest characters were based on pictures of concrete objects and the natural world (see below).

sun

moon

man

river

mountain

More complicated concepts are expressed by combinations of characters, some representing meanings, and some the way the word is pronounced.

Systems of romanisation (transcribing characters into the Latin or Western alphabet) have been devised for Chinese. The one promoted by the People's Republic of China is *pīnyīn*, a phonetic spelling of the sounds of Mandarin.

Nǐ Hǎo! is Mandarin for 'hello', and the title of a Dutch television course in spoken Chinese for beginners.

Chinese is what is known as a tone language. In Mandarin there are four tones, each of which can give a different meaning to a word. The tones are traditionally called high,

There are an estimated 60 000 characters in existence, though less than 2400 account for 99 per cent of actual usage. Traditionally, Chinese was written in columns and read from top to bottom. Today, the policy is to write horizontally from left to right.

high-rising, falling-rising and falling. For example, *mài* with a falling tone means 'sell', and *măi* with a falling-rising tone means 'buy'.

Chinese has many special features which make learning it a very different experience from learning a European language, and one that inevitably requires more time and effort. However, it has none of the grammatical complexity common to many European languages and you can, without too much difficulty, acquire enough basic spoken Chinese, using romanisation as a learning tool, to get by in China. Fewer up-to-date course materials are available in the United Kingdom for learning Chinese than for many of the other languages featured here. However, it's worthwhile contacting CILT (p. 176), who publish a list of courses and course books for learning Chinese.

THE 'LINGO' INDEX FOR CHINESE

	Easy	Hard
Pronunciation	■■■■■■■■■■■■■■■	□
Grammar	■■■■	□□□□□□□□□□
Writing and spelling	■■■■■■■■■■■■■■■	□
Vocabulary	■■■■■■■■■■■■	□□□
Reading	■■■■■■■■■■■■	□□□
Overall rating	■■■■■■■■■■■■	□□□□

Chinese pronunciation is very difficult for English speakers. Chinese has a lot of sounds that don't appear in English, and it's hard for English speakers to tell the difference between them, and harder still to pronounce them properly. Chinese also uses tones to distinguish words which are identical in other respects.

Chinese grammar is relatively simple. It doesn't have any of the complex endings that you get in European languages, and the word order is not very different from that of English. You'll sometimes find that the same word can serve as a noun, a verb or an adjective, though, and sometimes this can make it difficult to understand Chinese.

Chinese writing is hard for English speakers. If you want to get started, it might be worthwhile learning to read *pīnyīn* before you start reading the characters. It represents the sounds of Chinese in Roman letters, and is a good starting-point. However, even in *pīnyīn*, you'll find that the letters are used in a way that is unfamiliar to English speakers. It's easy to fall into the trap of pronouncing Chinese the way it's written in *pīnyīn*, instead of the way it ought to sound.

Chinese isn't related to any European language, and hasn't borrowed many words from English, so you will find few words that you can recognise easily. The problem of learning vocabulary in Chinese is made worse by the tone problem, and by the fact that words tend to be shorter than they are in English, so that it's easy to muddle up ones which sound similar.

Ann Nelson

Ann Nelson teaches English as a foreign language. She's 40. The school that she works for was asked to send a team of teachers to China, to run a 4-week training course for Chinese teachers. Ann decided that she ought to learn a bit of Chinese as a courtesy to her hosts. 'You can't really be an expert on language-teaching, and then not make an effort to learn the language of the country you're visiting,' she says.

Ann didn't have much advance notice of her visit, only 4 weeks, so she decided to be realistic about her aims. 'I would have liked to learn lots of Chinese, but I just didn't have the time. I knew I could reckon on about half an hour a day for a month – better than nothing, but still not very much. I bought a short survival course in Chinese, and I reckoned that would teach me basic greetings, and some useful phrases.'

Ann's course consisted of five half-hour lessons. The first lesson was pronunciation practice. She had some experience teaching Chinese students, so she already knew that Chinese was a tone language – the way your voice rises and falls when you say a syllable can change the meaning of what you say. 'Chinese students are always telling jokes about foreigners who get the wrong tone, and end up saying something quite different from what they really meant – usually something rude and embarrassing.' Chinese also has a lot of sounds that English doesn't use – what sounds like several different types of 's', 'z' and 'sh', and a set of unusual vowel sounds – so it's a difficult language for English speakers to pronounce.

The first lesson was almost completely devoted to practising these tones and the new sounds, and Ann found it a complete turn-off. 'To be honest,' she says, 'I think I've got a pretty good ear, but I just couldn't hear the differences. The voice on the tape would say two words that were supposed to be different, and I just couldn't tell them apart. At first, I thought it might be the personal stereo I was using. It wasn't an expensive model, and I thought it might not be good enough. I got a much better sound quality on a cassette player I borrowed from work, but I still couldn't hear the differences reliably.'

Ann eventually decided that it wasn't a good idea to spend a lot of time on the pronunciation lesson, but made a note to go back to it later when she had some basic knowledge of Chinese, and see if it made more sense then.

'The real lessons were much more interesting. The second lesson taught me greetings and useful expressions, and I used to make a point of trying them out with my students whenever I could. They were very helpful, and obviously got a lot of fun out of correcting the way I said things. I think they enjoyed being teachers instead of learners for a change.'

Ann's course came with a little booklet. This had some simple exercises in it, but they were really only extensions of the tape, and Ann didn't find them much help.

Apart from the first lesson with the sounds and tones, Ann planned to listen to each lesson five times. She found that she learned a lot of new things the first time through each lesson, but had trouble fixing them in her mind. 'It was really funny when you got to the end of the tape,' she says. 'The voice says, "Now you know enough Chinese to be able to change traveller's cheques and to buy a meal in a restaurant", and I knew it was completely unrealistic! A lot of people must feel really discouraged by this sort of thing. I knew that I'd have to listen to the tapes several times to fix things in my mind.'

Ann would have been glad to listen to the tapes a lot more, but she found that they contained too much English. They spent a lot of time explaining things slowly in English – Ann worked out that there was about four times as much English on the tapes as there was Chinese. 'That was OK the first time round,' she says, 'but by the time I'd listened to the explanations twice I practically knew them off by heart, and I felt it was just a waste of time listening to them again and again. I think it would have been a lot better if they'd put these explanations in the booklet, and used the space on the tape to let me hear more Chinese.' She eventually made up a new tape for herself, by copying the original one on her stereo system. She cut out all the English explanations, and that left her with a shorter tape – each lesson was reduced to about 6 minutes, all in Chinese. 'It was a bit of an odd collection,' she says. 'Some of it was single words, some of it was dialogue, and some of it was half a conversation where I was supposed to fill in the missing bits. It wouldn't have made any sense if I'd not heard the original, of course, but really it was only to jog my memory.'

Ann found that she could listen to this shorter tape four or five times a day. After a while, the phrases and expressions formed themselves naturally in her head, even when she wasn't thinking about them deliberately.

Her experience in China wasn't quite what she had expected. 'I'd often been abroad before, but I'd never been anywhere where I could only speak a few phrases. The really big thing was not being able to read the writing at all. It meant that I hadn't got a clue what was going on around me. I couldn't read the signs, so I couldn't find the way out of a building, or where the loos were, or where to buy a ticket for a bus trip. It was completely alien. The people we were working for gave us a guide who spoke English, and she sorted out most of our day-to-day problems for us. We would never have been able to handle them on what we'd learned from the course.

'They called it "survival Chinese", but I don't think we'd have been able to survive on it. Survival courses are obviously aimed at people travelling in places where they are used to tourists, and once you get outside that pattern things aren't nearly so smooth.'

One of Ann's friends had warned her that she would feel very tired while she was working away from home. Ann wasn't just tired, she was exhausted, and slept far more than she would have done at home. At first, she put it down to jet lag, but when it went on and on, she realised that it must be due to the strain of not being able to communicate with other people easily and naturally. A lot of the time, she had an interpreter working with her, but even that sometimes added to the strain. 'It's a bit like asking a centipede to explain how it walks,' she says. 'When you do things in a language you take for granted, it's all automatic, and you don't have to think about what you are doing. When you are dealing with people

Top ten phrases

Whatever language you learn, you'll find the following words and phrases useful for getting by:

Good morning/Good evening	Please speak more slowly
Hello/Goodbye	Could you say that again/ repeat that please
Pleased to meet you/How are you?	What's this/that . . .? (in, e.g., French)
Please/. . . please	How do you say . . .? (in, e.g., Japanese)
Thank you (very much)	Cheers!/To your health

who only have simple English, you are constantly trying to make things as simple as you can. You have these funny conversations where you think that you have explained things and that they have understood. Then later on, it becomes clear that they didn't understand, but were too polite to let you know. My Chinese was OK as far as it went, but it was pretty basic. There was one night when our bus broke down, and we got back to the hotel really late. I'd learned the words for "breakdown" and "bus" quite by chance, so I could give the hotel people an idea why we were late, but negotiating a dinner under these circumstances was way beyond me.'

Ann's verdict on her course? 'It was well worth the effort to learn some Chinese. I was surprised how well I managed in the areas the course had covered, considering how little time I'd had. For instance, I managed to change traveller's cheques in the bank without any bother – but that's the sort of thing you only do once, and I suppose I could have done it with sign language if I'd needed to. It was the ordinary everyday situations that I found really hard to deal with, not the touristy ones. If I was doing it again, though, I think I'd make more effort to pick up a bigger vocabulary. You can't really get by on 100 phrases, whatever the advertisements tell you. I'd certainly learn to read basic signs and public notices, even if I couldn't manage anything else. The few phrases I had, made a big difference. Saying *"Nǐ Hǎo!"* to people always raised a smile, and helped the atmosphere of my classes a lot. I'm not sure I got the tones right, but it seemed to work.'

What kind of a language-learner are you?

Imagine that you are in Ann Nelson's situation. You've been sent to China for 4 weeks, and you are anxious to learn some Chinese while you are there.

Answer the questions below by ticking one of the boxes alongside each of the statements, to show whether you agree or disagree with it.

SA = strongly agree
A = agree but not strongly
N = neither agree nor disagree
D = disagree
SD = strongly disagree

	SA	A	N	D	SD
1 I'd watch television in order to improve my Chinese.	☐	☐	☐	☐	☐
2 I'd only talk to someone if they spoke to me first.	☐	☐	☐	☐	☐
3 If I couldn't think of the right word I'd find some other way.	☐	☐	☐	☐	☐

	SA	A	N	D	SD
4 If I needed to get some stamps, I'd get a friend to buy them for me.	☐	☐	☐	☐	☐
5 It wouldn't bother me if people didn't always understand me in Chinese.	☐	☐	☐	☐	☐
6 I wouldn't try to use my Chinese in the English language classes I teach.	☐	☐	☐	☐	☐
7 It wouldn't bother me if people were speaking Chinese around me.	☐	☐	☐	☐	☐
8 I'd prefer to spend time with other English speakers.	☐	☐	☐	☐	☐
9 With a stranger, I'd always talk a bit of Chinese.	☐	☐	☐	☐	☐
10 I'd be embarrassed talking Chinese to someone I knew spoke English.	☐	☐	☐	☐	☐
11 It would be an unusual day if I didn't speak Chinese to anybody.	☐	☐	☐	☐	☐
12 I'd only speak Chinese if I knew I could get it absolutely right.	☐	☐	☐	☐	☐

How to score your answers

For the odd-numbered questions, score:

5 points for each SA answer
4 points for each A answer
3 points for each N answer
2 points for each D answer
1 point for each SD answer

For the even-numbered questions, score:

1 point for each SA answer
2 points for each A answer
3 points for each N answer
4 points for each D answer
5 points for each SD answer

What your score means
This quiz is designed to work out how you feel about communicating with other people when you are a long way from being really fluent.

35–60 points
You're a good language-learner, probably one of those people who always finds opportunities to practise with native speakers. Good language-learners enjoy being with a group of them, even if they can only understand a few words here and there. They don't sit at home, minding their own business – they get out and about, even if it means negotiating their own bus tickets. They ask the way to a place, even if they know where it is, just to get the satisfaction of recognising a few key words in the answers. They make three separate shopping trips, instead of just one, so that they can say 'hello' three times, instead of once. They watch television programmes that they wouldn't be seen dead watching in English, just to get familar with the kind of language that's

used in them. Then they try it out on their colleagues, or anyone else who will listen to them.

21–34 points

If you scored less than 35, don't worry. Not everybody wants to spend their lives learning foreign languages. Many people feel shy and embarrassed trying to speak in front of native speakers. Most people feel uncomfortable when they are surrounded by people talking in a language they don't know. Many people get a sense of panic when they know that they've got to negotiate something in a foreign language with someone who has no English at all. Still, you could have a look at the odd-numbered statements in the quiz to see the sort of thing that good language-learners do, and possibly copy one or two of the less alarming suggestions.

0–20 points

If you scored less than 20 points, you're going to have some problems learning your foreign language. Perhaps you're just shy. Or perhaps you are uncomfortable in situations where you think you might look a bit silly. Either way, you don't seem to be really interested in using your language to communicate with other people. The best thing you can do is make a resolution to use your foreign language with someone else at least once a day, even if it hurts at first.

Remember

★ Don't expect too much from a survival course. A few useful phrases can be helpful in breaking the ice, and will always be appreciated.

★ Use the materials you've got imaginatively. If the course doesn't do quite what you expected, see if you can tailor it to your own needs.

★ The more you use your language, the more you'll learn. Good language-learners are intrepid!

GOING NATIVE! Arabic

Profile: Tom Wray
Language for travel, Avoiding drop-out, Standards

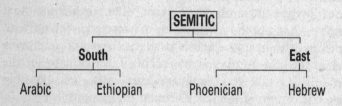

Simplified Semitic language family.

About Arabic

> **Arabic** is spoken by over 180 million people in the follow-
> ing areas: in Algeria, Bahrain, Djibouti, Egypt, Iraq, Jor-
> dan, Kuwait, Lebanon, Libya, Mauritania, Morocco,
> Oman, Qatar, Saudi Arabia, Somalia, Sudan, Syria,
> Tunisia, United Arab Emirates, North Yemen, South
> Yemen, Palestine.
>
> Arabic is also the mother tongue of the Palestinian
> Arabs in Israel and of some groups in south-west Iran and
> Soviet Central Asia.
>
> It is the language of the sacred book of Islam, the Koran
> (Qur'an), and as such is also learned by many millions of
> Moslems throughout the world. Because of its importance
> as a world language, Arabic has been adopted as one of the
> official languages of the United Nations Organization.

There are basically two kinds of Arabic: literary and spoken.

Literary Arabic is used as the written medium throughout the Arab world, and is spoken on formal occasions – in speeches, sermons, news broadcasts, and so on. For all everyday purposes – at home, in shops and offices, cafés and restaurants – colloquial Arabic is used.

The Arab world is so vast that, hardly surprisingly, the spoken language varies from country to country, region to region: a Moroccan may not understand an Iraqi at all. Most modern courses in spoken Arabic, however, choose the Arabic of Egypt as a standard: geographically and historically it lies at the heart of the Arab world; its population (50 million) far exceeds that of any other Arab country; and practically everyone in the Arab world is exposed to Egyptian Arabic through films, radio, popular songs and television soap operas. It is therefore generally held to be the most prestigious spoken variety of Arabic. Whichever Arab country you visit, you will find people can understand and adapt to Egyptian Arabic. Non-Egyptian words can easily be added to this basic knowledge.

The Arabic alphabet
Arabic belongs to the Semitic group of languages, and uses a cursive script which is written from right to left. The alphabet consists of 28 letters, and is often seen, unnecessarily, as a barrier to learning the language.

Arabs are rightly proud of the beauty of the Arabic script. Varieties of this script are used to write Farsi, Urdu, Malay and many other languages.

Beginners in the spoken language may, however, prefer to approach it through a romanised version, such as the one suggested overleaf. Most sounds in Arabic are, in fact, similar to those found in English (with a few exceptions), though it's as well to remember that traditional Arab script is composed of consonants only. Texts for beginners usually incorporate a system of vowel signs to help with pronunciation.

kh	H	j or g	th	t	b	a	'glottal stop
خ	ح	ج	ث	ت	ب	أ	ء

D	S	sh	s	z	r	th	d
ض	ص	ش	س	ز	ر	ذ	د

k	q	f	gh	ع	Z	T
ك	ق	ف	غ	ع	ظ	ط

y	w	h	n	m	l
ي	و	هـ	ن	م	ل

These three letters are used as long vowels:
aa ا   ii ي *or* ـي   uu و

The glottal stop ء is usually 'carried' on top of one
of the long vowel symbols; eg أ = 'a

See if you can decipher the names of these countries. They
are all transcribed from Arabic. Spot the odd one out: one of
them is a capital city, not a country. Which one?

1 ilbaHreen   4 libnaan   7 ilqaahira
2 ilƐiraa   5 muritaanya   8 issuƐudiyya
3 ilkuweet   6 Ɛumaan   9 tuunis
                                10 issudaan

Answers are at the base of the page.

Arabic speakers are used to hearing a wide variety of accents
from within the Arab world and, like people in many other
cultures, are genuinely delighted to find a foreigner making an
effort to speak their language. They are more than forgiving if
you make mistakes in pronunciation or grammar.

The odd one out is Cairo.
1 Bahrain 2 Iraq 3 Kuwait 4 Lebanon 5 Mauritania
6 Oman 7 Cairo 8 Saudi Arabia 9 Tunisia 10 Sudan

136

The major, and official, language of Iran is Persian, or Farsi. It is spoken by the majority of Iran's population of almost 50 million people. Persian is also the second official language of Afghanistan, and is widely spoken in the Soviet provinces of Tadjikistan and Turkestan. It belongs to the Indo-European group of languages, though it uses a cursive script written from right to left, and has borrowed lots of words from Arabic.

Materials for learning Arabic in the United Kingdom are of variable quality and not always readily available. There are a number of specialist bookshops who may be able to help. Try also contacting the cultural attaché at the embassy of the country you're interested in.

THE 'LINGO' INDEX FOR **ARABIC**

	Easy		Hard
Pronunciation	■■■■■■□□□□□□□□□		
Grammar	■■■■■■■■■■□□□□□		
Writing and spelling	■■■■■■■■■■■□□□□		
Vocabulary	■■■■■■■■■■■□□□□		
Reading	■■■■■■■■■■■■■■□		
Overall rating	■■■■■■■■■■■□□□□□		

Arabic pronunciation doesn't present a lot of difficulties for English speakers. Arabic uses a set of consonant sounds that are made right in the back of your throat. These don't appear in English, but are fairly easy to learn. In any case, Arabic varies from one country to another, so its speakers are tolerant of accent differences.

Arabic grammar is hard for English speakers. There are two genders, and adjectives change their form depending on the gender of the nouns they go with, and on other features too. Plural forms are often irregular. Verbs are extremely complicated. There are four main types, each using different patterns to indicate different aspects of time. These changes don't involve just adding an ending here and there: they usually also involve a change in the middle of a word. Arabic also uses different forms depending on the sex of the speaker.

Arabic writing is basically alphabetic, but rather different from Roman letters. Letters have different shapes depending on whether they come at the beginning, middle or end of a word. Arabic written for adults leaves out the vowels, so the reader has to fill them in. Ts bt lk rdng ths srt f txt n Nglsh, bt lt hrdr bcs f th w th wrds wrk. (And don't forget it goes from right to left as well.)

Arabic vocabulary isn't systematically related to vocabulary in any European language, though if you speak Spanish you may be able to recognise some words. Arabic words are very different from English ones. Most of them are based on a *root* consisting of three consonants. You can build up whole families of words by putting different combinations of vowels into this framework. So, for instance, you get the root **k-t-b,** and on this framework you can build: **katab** – he wrote; **yktib** – he writes; **kaatib** – clerk; **kataba** – clerks; **kitaab** – book; **kutub** – books; **maktuub** – written; **maktab** – office; **maktaba** – library; and so on. This makes it quite hard to understand basic Arabic words, but once you get used to the patterns it doesn't take long to build up a big vocabulary.

Tom Wray

Tom Wray is 25 and lives in London. He first became interested in Arabic when he watched *Lawrence of Arabia* as a teenager. 'It was a case of love at first sight,' he says. 'As soon as I could, I went off on an adventure holiday, driving across the Sahara, and I've been doing it every year since then.'

The first time he went on holiday to North Africa, it didn't occur to Tom to learn any Arabic, but once he got there, he realised it had been a mistake. A lot of people spoke English, of course, but not nearly as many as he had expected, and it was obvious that he was missing out on a lot because he could only speak English. If he'd spoken French, that might have been a help, but he didn't.

'When I got back to Britain, I decided I needed to go to an evening class. I thought I'd be able to find an Arabic class easily enough. Every autumn we used to get a free newspaper that listed all sorts of classes, and I remembered that a lot of them were beginners' classes in languages. When it arrived, though, there wasn't any Arabic – only French and Spanish and other European languages.'

Tom checked with his local library, and they found a course for him run by the local polytechnic. Tom was a bit scared by this – he was expecting a polytechnic course to be high-powered – and was surprised to find that everyone was a beginner, just like him. The class was fairly small, though; only eight people turned up to the first meeting. One person dropped out after 2 weeks, and the teacher said that if the numbers dropped to six the class would have to be cancelled.

At first, Tom didn't enjoy the classes at all. The class was using a *Get by in Arabic* course, which was just what he needed, but because there were so few people, the teacher made a point of getting everyone to do all the exercises out loud, one at a time. Tom wasn't happy with this. He felt that the other students were all better than he was. He was scared to open his mouth in case he made a mistake and people laughed at him, and as the work got more difficult, the problems he had in class also got more difficult. In the end, Tom could feel himself breaking into a sweat when he knew it was getting to his turn.

After 6 weeks, Tom nearly packed it all in, but he was persuaded by the other students to keep going. 'We talked about it in the pub after the class,' he says. 'I thought I was useless, and everybody else was brilliant. It turned out that I wasn't the only one who thought he was stupid. Almost everyone else felt the same about themselves. If we hadn't talked about it, we would all have given up because we thought we weren't any good.'

Not everyone is a gifted language-learner. Lots of learners find classes hard to cope with, especially if they were early school-leavers, or if they haven't been to classes for many years. A large proportion of language classes fold because of drop-outs, and a lot of this can be put down to people feeling uncomfortable.

Not all classes are run like Tom's one, though, and if you are an anxious, unconfident learner, you might be lucky enough to find an alternative class that suits you better. Most people think that learning a language involves talking a lot, and expect their classes to include a high proportion of conversation. But if you watch the way little children learn to talk, you'll notice that really young ones don't say anything at all for about 18 months. This is partly because they haven't learned to separate speech from the rest of the things they hear around them, and partly because they don't have the words to express themselves. Mostly, though, it's because it's more efficient to learn a language by listening to it rather than by speaking it.

In most language classes, teachers encourage you to talk as much as you can, as quickly as you can. They'll often do this by asking you to listen to something and then repeat it, or to listen to something and repeat it with a slight change. Most learners find this kind of exercise incredibly hard. When you are a beginner, even three or four words can be too much.

Your memory just has too much work to do, and you freeze up completely. If this happens a lot in class, it can be depressing.

People are now beginning to think that it might not necessarily be a good idea for learners to talk in the foreign language right from the start. Instead, you should spend a long time just listening quietly. Saying nothing for weeks on end probably isn't a good idea for most adult learners – it will drive your teacher crazy for a start! But it is a good idea to wait until speaking feels natural and you can do it without stress. You might need to have a word with your teacher if you have problems.

If you try to talk before you're really ready, you'll be struggling with the words, the sounds and the grammar at the same time. You can't possibly get them all right at first. The few bits you get wrong can sometimes seem much more important than the others that you get right, which can make you frustrated and disappointed. When that happens, you're well on the way to dropping out of a course. The secret to success is not to expect too much of yourself. Just push yourself a bit further every time you get the chance to use the language – but don't expect to get it all right all the time.

Once Tom got over his anxiety about talking, things went much better for him, but he still found that the class wasn't really going in the direction he wanted. He thought that it concentrated rather a lot on speaking correct Arabic, whereas he was interested in something a bit more informal – the kind of Arabic you'd need on a trek across the Sahara. Nor was he really interested in learning to read and write Arabic, although he knew he needed enough to read signs and directions.

He then discovered that one of his local video shops kept a stock of Arabic videos, and started to hire them out at the weekends. They were often set in the desert, and many involved long journeys by camel, with just a few characters talking to each other. 'It wasn't quite like the treks we did,' says Tom, 'but the similarities were there. I didn't always understand what was happening – the films didn't have subtitles as they would have had on television – but you could get the idea just from watching the pictures. In each film there was some word or phrase where the meaning was obvious, and it just stuck in my mind, even if I hadn't heard it before. If I watched the film a couple of times, instead of just once, it was even better.'

Tom was also interested in the films because they showed aspects of life that he didn't learn about in his class. 'There were always lots of pictures of people eating, so you could see how they sat, and how they often used their fingers to eat, and what to do with coffee, and things like that. And you could see how close people stood to each other, and how the men touch each other in a way we don't – I'd noticed that in North Africa the first time I went on a trek. I used to ask the teacher about these things. He'd say, "Oh yes, we always do it like that," but he never explained unless we asked him. I suppose he just took it for granted.'

At the end of the year, Tom went off on another expedition to North Africa. 'It made a heck of a difference being able to speak Arabic,' he says. 'I wasn't fluent, but I'd worked hard at the class, and done the homework, and watched the videos, and my teacher said I had a pretty good vocabulary for a beginner. I still wasn't as good as some of the people in the class, but that didn't bother me in the end. I knew that I'd done one trek without any Arabic at all, so on the next one I was bound to be better. The really good thing was the way speaking Arabic helped me make friends with the local guides. I don't suppose it amounted to much, but just being able to ask someone what his name was in Arabic, and offer him a cigarette, made me feel less like a tourist – and that's what it was all about.

'I'd still like to know how Lawrence of Arabia did it.'

What kind of a language-learner are you?

Are you heading for a drop-out? This quiz will teach you how to look for warning signs, and what to do about them.

Read each of the statements, and tick one of the boxes alongside it, to show whether you agree or disagree with it.

SA = strongly agree
A = agree
N = neither agree nor disagree
D = disagree
SD = strongly disagree.

	SA	A	N	D	SD
1 I worry a lot about making mistakes in class.	☐	☐	☐	☐	☐
2 I only talk in class if I know I can get it right.	☐	☐	☐	☐	☐
3 I think I'm one of the worst students in my class.	☐	☐	☐	☐	☐
4 I think I'm holding the rest of the class back.	☐	☐	☐	☐	☐
5 I only talk in class if the teacher asks me something.	☐	☐	☐	☐	☐

	SA	A	N	D	SD

6 I'm always glad if the teacher doesn't ask me to give an answer. ☐ ☐ ☐ ☐ ☐

7 I'm afraid people will laugh at me when I get things wrong in class. ☐ ☐ ☐ ☐ ☐

8 I hate role-play exercises when you can't avoid talking with other students. ☐ ☐ ☐ ☐ ☐

9 I always end up trembling if I have to talk in class. ☐ ☐ ☐ ☐ ☐

10 I don't usually know the answers to the questions the teacher asks. ☐ ☐ ☐ ☐ ☐

11 When it's my turn to answer a question I break out in a sweat. ☐ ☐ ☐ ☐ ☐

12 I think my class is going too fast for me. ☐ ☐ ☐ ☐ ☐

How to score your answers

Score:
5 points for each SA answer
4 points for each A answer
3 points for each N answer
2 points for each D answer
1 point for each SD answer

What your score means
The statements in the quiz are the sort of comments made by students who end up dropping out of language courses. The more strongly you agree with them, the more likely it is that you will be a drop-out too.

48–60 points
This is the danger zone. You agreed with almost all the statements in this quiz, and probably recognised bits of yourself in Tom Wray's profile. You really want to learn your language, but find the classes are torture, rather than fun. If you're serious about carrying on, you'll have to take some corrective action quickly.

There are two things you have to do. First, talk to the teacher and explain how anxious you feel in class. You probably imagine he thinks you are completely useless. It's more likely that he's not aware of your difficulties, and that he thinks you're just like the other students. Ask him to make things easier for you in class. He might not want to let you off the hook completely, but he might be willing to ask you easier questions until you build up your self-confidence.

Second, you need to learn to take more risks. Deep down, you're afraid of making mistakes because you think it makes you look stupid, and as long as you feel like that you'll always be embarrassed about talking in a foreign language. Everyone feels stupid when they know only a few dozen halting expressions. Good language-learners are able to shrug it off, though, and laugh at themselves when they get things wrong. Start off by making an effort to volunteer in class, instead of waiting for the teacher to ask you. Give yourself a reward for every class in which you volunteer at least one answer, and give yourself an especially big reward if you volunteered when you weren't sure the answer was correct.

25–47 points
Most people fall into this category. Language classes make you a bit anxious, but no more than any other class. You could improve your score by learning to be more adventurous, and pushing yourself a bit harder. Try asking the teacher questions, instead of waiting for him to ask you.

12–24 points
Language classes hold no terrors for you – why don't you keep an eye open for people who aren't as confident as you are, and give them a helping hand in class?

Remember
★ A class can teach you the language, but you also need to learn about the culture. You might have to take this initiative yourself.

★ Don't let yourself get tense about your language classes. You'll learn faster if you are relaxed.

★ Don't underestimate the power of listening to help you learn a language.

GOING BADLY? Urdu

Profile: Sharon Browne
Evening classes, Becoming fluent, Unblocking blocks

About community languages

Over 160 languages are used in Britain by ethnic minority communities. Collectively, they are frequently referred to as 'community languages'.

These include German, Italian, Greek, Spanish and Cantonese, but the majority of immigrants in the United Kingdom speak one of the 16 official languages of India.

South Asian communities who have come from the subcontinent speak mainly Bengali, Gujarati, Hindi, Punjabi and Urdu.

Hindi-Urdu is the lingua franca of South Asians, though the younger generation (and some of the older generation too) also uses English to overcome linguistic and ethnic boundaries. Like Urdu, Hindi has been adopted by many non-native speakers as the community language for their children.

The main Indian languages belong to the Indo-European family. This means they are related, however distantly, to English, and are relatively easy languages for Europeans to learn.

Most radio and television programmes for Asians settled in Britain are, like the great majority of the films produced in India, in Hindi-Urdu.

The main community languages in the United Kingdom are Hindi, Urdu, Bengali, Gujarati and Punjabi.

Hindi
★ National language of India
★ First or second language for over 300 million people
★ Written in Devanagari script

Urdu
★ National language of Pakistan
★ Spoken by 85 million on the Indian subcontinent as an official language
★ Written in a form of Arabic script

In their everyday spoken forms, Hindi and Urdu are almost identical. This form is called Hindi by non-Muslims and Urdu by Muslims. Hindi-Urdu is the first or second language of Indian and Pakistani settlers in Britain. It is now probably the most commonly spoken language in the United Kingdom after English.

Bengali
★ Official language of Bangladesh
★ Spoken by over 140 million people

Gujarati
★ One of 16 official languages of India
★ Spoken by 35 million people

Punjabi
★ The language of the Punjab (pronounced 'panjabi', not 'poonjabi')
★ Spoken by over 70 million on the Indian subcontinent
★ Closely identified with the Sikh community
★ Written in Gurmukhi script

Speakers of Bengali, Gujarati and Punjabi use Hindi-Urdu as a link language (with English) to communicate.

Publishers and broadcasters are now beginning to provide up-to-date material for adults as well as children to learn Indian and other community languages. These languages are being seen as an increasingly interesting and useful option by those whose personal or professional lives bring them into contact with speakers of these languages, especially by health workers, social workers and teachers.

For more information, contact the Indian High Commission, the National Council for Mother Tongue Teaching, or your local education authority's adviser for multicultural education.

THE 'LINGO' INDEX FOR **URDU**

	Easy	Hard
Pronunciation	■■■■■■□□□□□□□□
Grammar	■■■■■□□□□□□□□□
Writing and spelling	■■■■■■■■■■■■■□□□
Vocabulary	■■■■■■■■■□□□□□
Reading	■■■■■■■■■■■■■■□□
Overall rating	■■■■■■■■■■□□□□□

Many people think that Urdu is a hard language to learn, but in many ways it's a lot easier than French or German. An added advantage is that there are plenty of native speakers in Britain and plenty of Asian video shops, supermarkets and newsagents.

Urdu pronunciation is fairly easy for English speakers, partly because we have good stereotypes of the way Urdu speakers sound. The main points to watch out for are:

★ Urdu has a set of consonant sounds that you make by

bending your tongue backwards to touch the roof of your mouth.

★ Urdu has a systematic distinction between breathy consonants and consonants that aren't breathy. This distinction is hard for English speakers to notice, though not hard to produce once they are used to it.

★ Urdu has a set of nasal vowels (a bit like French vowels).

Urdu grammar isn't especially difficult. The main point is that verbs come at the end of a sentence and adjectives and, usually, prepositions come after their nouns. There are no articles, but nouns are classified by gender, and adjectives sometimes change their form according to the gender of the noun they go with.

Urdu vocabulary is partly Indo-European, and partly Arabic in origin. This means that you will be able to recognise some cognate words, but not as many as you would in a language like Spanish.

Sharon Browne

Sharon Browne is a primary school teacher. She's 29. Many of the children she teaches come from homes where English isn't the first language. There are 30 children in her class, and 24 of them are bilingual. 'By the time they come to me,' she says, 'most of them speak English really well, but I often have problems when I have to deal with the parents.'

Sharon wanted to be able to talk to the parents. 'I was a bit naïve about it at first,' she says. 'I didn't know anything about the languages my kids spoke. I knew there were Sikhs and Moslems and Hindus, because they all eat different things for religious reasons, but I hadn't really thought about the languages at all.' Sharon went along to her local library, and asked about courses in Hindi. There weren't any – but the librarian explained that she might be better off learning Urdu, or Bengali, or Punjabi, or Gujarati or Tamil, depend-

Going badly?

ing on where she worked. Sharon eventually established that
most of the children in her class spoke Urdu, and she found
an evening class run by the local education authority. The
teacher was a native speaker, and also a primary school
teacher, so Sharon felt pretty much at home with her, and
enjoyed the classes.

'The biggest problem for me was learning to read,' she
says. 'Urdu uses an alphabet that's based on Arabic writing,
and it's very different from English. For a start, it goes from
right to left, instead of from left to right, and the letters
aren't always the same shape – they change depending on
whether they are at the beginning of the word, in the middle
or at the end. Even worse, in Urdu writing, you don't write
down everything you hear: you write the consonants, but the
vowels are often left out. It makes it hard to read.'

Sharon would have been quite happy just learning to talk
in Urdu, but her teacher said it was important for her to learn
to read as well if she wanted to get really fluent. They spent a
lot of time in class just drawing the letters, and learning to
read simple words. Sharon learned how to write the names of
the children in her class first. She found that much easier
than learning the letters on their own, and since they were
words that she already knew and needed to use, she could
practise them every day, without it becoming a chore.

Sharon's teacher told the evening class that it was important to be able to read quickly. Once they could recognise
and write the basic letters, she got them to make up a list of
50 words and write each one on a file card in big letters.
Then, each day, they had to read all 50 cards, and time how
long it took them. At first, Sharon read the words letter by
letter but, pretty soon, she was able to take them in at a
glance, and could read them quickly. 'Timing how quickly I
could read these cards helped me realise that I really was
making progress,' she says.

Sharon went to the beginners' class for a year. At the end
of it, she felt she had learned a lot. She could read and write

basic Urdu, and could hold simple conversations with the parents. She could buy her groceries from the corner shop, which was run by an Urdu speaker.

She decided she'd like to get really fluent, and signed up for a more advanced class.

'The main difference between the elementary class and the advanced class was that you needed to know a lot more words,' she says. 'The teacher said that you could get by with about 2000 basic words, but needed a lot more to be really fluent. She told us that the best way of picking up a big vocabulary was reading, and she used to set us lots of reading homework every week.'

Sharon's teacher gave them simple story-books to start with. She told them to read through them with a marker pen, and mark each word they didn't know and couldn't guess. When they'd marked 20 words they had to stop, and look the words up in a dictionary. They then wrote each of these words down in a notebook, along with its meaning in English, and a couple of other Urdu words that were connected with it. At first, Sharon found that she could barely manage four or five lines of her story. It was really hard work. 'The teacher told us to get a big sheet of paper and put it up on the wall. Every day we had to mark on it how much we had managed to read before we'd reached our 20 words. At first, I could only get through four or five lines, and when I drew my graph it looked really pathetic. After a bit, though, it suddenly started to take off, and I found I could manage 20 or 30 lines. I was looking up less than one word in every line, and I felt really great.'

Sharon also used her vocabulary book for revision. She noticed that words she'd found hard when she first met them, were often easy when she went back to them – she usually remembered words she'd seen more than once, but she often forgot ones she'd only seen once. Her teacher told her it probably wasn't worthwhile making a special effort to learn words like that – they were useful ones to recognise, but she probably wouldn't want to use them.

'When I'd been using my notebook for a month, it had just over 500 words in it. The teacher told us to go through the notebook, crossing out the words we knew without having to think about them. My first notebook came to 220 words I knew really well. Then we had to make another wall chart that showed how many words we had collected from our notebooks, and every month we added the totals up and drew the new total on the chart.

'These were just the sort of tricks I would have used with my kids in school, but it certainly helped me realise that I was making progress. Every time I looked at the charts on the wall, I could see myself getting better.'

Sharon's teacher was also keen on showing her pupils that they were getting more fluent.

First, she showed them how to listen to the news in Urdu on their local radio station. She told them to listen to the announcer reading the news, and try to repeat aloud what he said. Sometimes, there was a bit that they just couldn't repeat, and every time this happened, they scored a point. They kept going until they had five points; the final score was how long they could keep going. Sharon found this really hard at first but, with practice, she could 'shadow' the news for almost 2 minutes before she came unstuck five times.

Next, the teacher gave them five picture postcards and a tape, and made them record themselves describing the pictures on the tape. It didn't matter what they said. She told them that they could describe what they saw in the pictures, or describe how they reacted to them. The important thing was just to keep talking, even when they were stuck for a word.

Sharon recorded herself describing the postcards every Sunday morning, for five minutes. Then she had to listen to the tape, and count the number of times she produced a long pause or a hesitation. The teacher suggested that she could give each hesitation a score – five points for a really long one, two for a shorter one, and one for a slight one – the exact details didn't much matter as long as she was consistent from week to week.

At first, Sharon's score was huge but, as she became more and more confident, the really long pauses when she couldn't think of anything to say gradually disappeared, and her score got better and better. She never reached a score of zero, of course, but most of her hesitations were quite short. She thought at first that it might just be because she was starting to get familiar with the postcards, but even when she got a new set of cards, although her score went up a bit, it soon came down again.

Sharon says: 'Some of my friends were doing evening classes in French and German, and said they were fed up because they couldn't tell if they were getting better. I didn't have that problem. You couldn't move in my kitchen for progress charts, and I could *see* I was getting better. The interesting thing was the way that I'd get stuck at one level, and then suddenly make a surge on to the next one, as if I'd forced my way round an obstacle. My teacher had us measuring lots of different things, and I was never completely stuck on everything at the same time. If I wasn't making any progress on the vocabulary, then I was probably getting better at describing the postcards.'

What kind of a language-learner are you?

Here's a quiz that we designed to help Sharon Browne think about learning Urdu. All the statements ask her to say how she feels about the language, and how she feels about Urdu speakers. If you're learning a different language, you'll have to change Urdu to French, German or whatever. Tick one of the boxes at the side of each statement, depending on whether you agree or disagree with it.

SA = strongly agree
A = agree but not strongly
N = neither agree nor disagree
D = disagree but not strongly
SD = strongly disagree

	SA	A	N	D	SD
1 On the whole, I like Urdu speakers a lot.	☐	☐	☐	☐	☐
2 I enjoy talking with Urdu speakers.	☐	☐	☐	☐	☐
3 I think Urdu speakers would respect me for learning to speak their language.	☐	☐	☐	☐	☐
4 It's a mark of respect to learn other people's language if you have to deal with them a lot.	☐	☐	☐	☐	☐
5 I'm interested in Urdu culture.	☐	☐	☐	☐	☐
6 I feel at ease with Urdu speakers.	☐	☐	☐	☐	☐
7 I think Urdu is a beautiful language.	☐	☐	☐	☐	☐
8 I'd like to live for a while in a country where they speak Urdu.	☐	☐	☐	☐	☐

	SA	A	N	D	SD

9 Being able to speak Urdu will help me understand people I live close to.

10 Speaking Urdu will let me help other people more than I can at the moment.

11 I don't like talking to Urdu speakers in English.

12 I'd make more effort to learn Urdu than to learn any other language.

How to score your answers

The questions in this quiz are designed to work out how closely you identify with the people who speak the language you are learning.

Score:
5 points for each SA answer
4 points for each A answer
3 points for each N answer
2 points for each D answer
1 point for each SD answer

What your score means

The more points you get, the more strongly you identify with the people who speak the language you are learning. If you scored 48 points or more, you identify very strongly with Urdu speakers (or French or German speakers). You would really like to become part of the community that speaks the language – perhaps you are considering marrying into it, or are planning to leave the United Kingdom to live abroad. You are very pleased when people take you for a native speaker, or when they compliment you on the way you talk. Indian take-aways aren't just a convenience for you, they're more a way of life.

Identifying with the community that speaks the language is a very good way of increasing your motivation to learn. People who want to become part of a community generally end up learning to speak the language very well, though it might take them a long time to get as fluent as they would really like to be. Those like Sharon, who identify strongly with a community, and want to become part of it, have many advantages. They will often join clubs where native speakers give classes or organise cultural events specially for learners. And they will usually make friends with a few native speakers, so that speaking the language becomes a natural part of their daily lives.

Most people aren't single-minded like this. You might even have scored less than 20 points in our quiz. This doesn't mean that you won't be any good at learning Urdu (or French or German). It just means that your motives for learning the language are different. Perhaps you work for a firm that exports to Pakistan, but you loathe hot climates and dislike hot food. When you're out there, you just can't wait to get back to fish and chips in rainy old Manchester.

Learning a language doesn't necessarily imply that you want to become part of the culture. But if you really like its speakers (or even just one of them) you won't give up when the going gets difficult.

Remember

★ You don't have to like the people whose language you are learning, but it helps a lot if you do.

★ If you don't identify with the people whose language you are learning, you'll need to find some other good reason for wanting to learn it.

★ Find ways of making your progress visible to you and your friends. You are probably making progress, even when you think you've come to a complete standstill.

GET UP AND GO! Greek

Profile: Louise Carter
Guessing and deducing, Links and roots, Language and people

About Greek

> **Greek** is spoken by over 10 million people in Greece itself.
> In overseas Greek communities (known as the 'Greek dia-
> spora') it's spoken by an additional three million people or
> more. After Athens, Melbourne is the world's largest
> Greek-speaking city!

The Greek alphabet

The word 'alphabet' is made up from the first two letters of
the ancient Greek alphabet: *alpha* (α) and *beta* (β). The
modern Greek alphabet consists of 24 letters, many of which
are the same as those of the Latin alphabet, based on Greek
and used in English and most other European languages.

Α Β Γ Δ Ε Ζ Η Θ Ι Κ Λ Μ
A V G D E Z E TH I K L M

Ν Ξ Ο Π Ρ Σ Τ Υ Φ Χ Ψ Ω
N KS O P R S T I PH CH PS O

The words listed overleaf are in common use in Greece.
Some are place names, others are shop and street signs or
drinks. See how many you can translate, using the key
above. Answers are at the base of the page.

Lingo!

1. ΚΑΦΕ	6. ΑΘΗΝΑ
2. ΚΑΦΕΝΕΙΟ	7. ΘΕΣΣΑΛΟΝΙΚΗ
3. ΤΑΒΕΡΝΑ	8. ΣΚΙΑΘΟΣ
4. ΜΠΑΡ	9. ΣΑΜΟΣ
5. ΟΥΖΟ	10. ΔΕΛΦΟΙ

There is no Greek letter 'b'. The sound 'b' is conveyed by the letters **ΜΠ**

Alphabets different from the one we're used to can sometimes seem an insurmountable barrier to learning another language (see also Japanese p. 87, Russian p. 110, Arabic p. 134). Often, however, it doesn't require nearly as much time and effort to get to grips with them as you might think.

Greek words in English

Many words in the English language have their roots in ancient Greek, and anyone learning modern Greek will come across words that may remind them of English ones. For example, if a Greek agrees with you he may say: *'simfoni!'* – 'Agreed!'. This is not far from the harmonious agreement of a 'symphony' (*sin* means 'together', and *phonos* means 'sound', and is also found – see later – in microphones and megaphones).

In Greece, a friend (*filos*) is a friend for life. It's also a word which forms the roots of other familiar words:

Philanthropy: love of man (*anthropos* – man)
Philology: the science of language (*logos* – word)
Philosophy: love of wisdom (*sofia* – wisdom)

---

1 coffee 2 kafeneíon: a café 3 taverna: a restaurant 4 bar 5 ouzo: aniseed-based aperitif 6 Athina: Athens 7 Thessaloníki: city in northern Greece 8 Skiathos 9 Samos 10 Delphi

Greek roots can either be for the good (*kalos* – good, beautiful) or bad (*kakos* – bad). While we may enjoy a symphony, we are less likely to appreciate a cacophony. Calligraphy, however, the art of fine writing, owes its roots to *kalos* and *grafo* (I write).

The verb *grafo* is also at the root of many other human activities:

Biography: a written account of another person's life (*bios* – life)
Autobiography: a person's life written by himself (*autos* – self)
Choreography: the art of arranging dances (*khoros* – dance)
Geography: the science describing the world (*geo* – earth, world)

If we are prone to exaggeration we may encounter the Greek word *megalos* (big, great): a megalomaniac is one who has delusions of grandeur; many megalomaniacs (or film directors) make use of a megaphone, especially when trying to communicate in a noisy, crowded megalopolis (*pólis* – city).

For other people, small (*mikros*) is beautiful:

A microphone intensifies tiny sounds.
A microscope magnifies minute objects, revealing the occasional microbe or even a microcosm (*kosmos* – world, people).

So, you can see that modern Greek is itself a microcosm of much of the vocabulary which will help us to learn other foreign languages, and some knowledge of the language, as well as being useful for ordering ouzo or retsina on a Greek island, may even help us to become a nation of polyglots: (*poly* – much, many; *glossa* – language)!

THE 'LINGO' INDEX FOR **GREEK**

	Easy	Hard
Pronunciation	■■■□□□□□□□□□□□□	
Grammar	■■■■■■■■□□□□□□□	
Writing and spelling	■■■■■■■■■■■■□□□	
Vocabulary	■■■■■□□□□□□□□□□	
Reading	■■■■■■■■□□□□□□□	
Overall rating	■■■■■■■■■□□□□□□	

Greek pronunciation is easy for English speakers. The sounds are all very straightforward.

The grammar is not too difficult either, if you're familiar with the way other European languages work. Word order is roughly the same as in English. Nouns come in three genders, and adjectives change their form depending on the gender of the noun that they go with. Nouns also change their form depending on their case, and this can also affect adjectives. Verbs change their form to mark different tenses.

Greek is written in a special alphabet. However, it's closely related to the Roman alphabet that we use, so many of the letter shapes will already be familiar. As we've seen, Greek writing is not a serious obstacle to learning the language.

Greek vocabulary is really easy for English speakers. A very large number of words are directly related to English, and it's possible to build up a large vocabulary pretty quickly by systematically exploiting these connections.

Louise Carter

Louise Carter is 45, and married to Geoff, who is 10 years older than she is. Geoff was given the chance of early retirement, and the two of them have decided that they would really like to live in a warm climate for a few years. They bought a plot of land in Cyprus, and are having a house built there.

Louise says, 'Moving to the Mediterranean sounds really exotic, but it's much more common than you'd imagine. Geoff travelled to Greece and Cyprus because of his job, and he knows the area quite well. He's not much good at languages though – we lived in Brussels for 10 years, but his French is pretty awful. I'm the one that will have to learn Greek.'

Louise tried to join a Greek class, but there wasn't anything suitable – only one on New Testament Greek, and she didn't fancy that. But one day, she noticed in her local library an advertisement from a Greek native speaker offering to give one-to-one classes in Greek in exchange for English lessons. She gave her a ring, and they arranged to

---

Modern Greek is directly descended from the ancient language. Though there have been many changes along the way, the ancient Greek of Homer and Sophocles is still accessible to speakers of modern Greek. In Greece today, however, you'll come across not one, but two languages: **katharevousa** and **dimotiki**.

Katharevousa is an official, artificial ('pure') version of ancient Greek, and was for a long time the language of officialdom, used in newspapers, in some literature and in schools and universities.

Dimotiki is the natural spoken language, and was officially adopted as Greece's national language following the end of the dictatorship of 1967–74. You'll still see many signs in Greece written in *katharevousa*, while the spoken, demotic word is quite different. A Greek will ask for *psomi* (bread) from the *fournos* (oven, bakery), but the sign over the baker's will often read: *artopiion* (from *artos*, the ancient Greek word for 'bread').

---

meet twice a week in a nearby café: English on Mondays, Greek on Wednesdays.

'It was quite hard going,' Louise says. 'I'd had plenty of experience learning languages before, but I'd never tried to teach one. Maria's English was much better than my Greek, and a lot of the questions she asked me were details of what words meant in English. Often they were things I hadn't really thought much about. With me, she spent a lot of time helping me to read the Greek alphabet, and learning very basic expressions. I think I'd imagined we'd just start having conversations, as we used to in formal classes, but it's much harder working one-to-one, especially when you're a real beginner.'

Louise found that she didn't get much out of her classes at first, and she certainly couldn't have learned fluent Greek that way. She did a lot of homework, though, working systematically through a course book, and found it very useful to have a native speaker to help her. Maria used to mark the exercises she did, and could tell her why answers she thought were right weren't always the same as the ones the textbook provided. Maria was also able to tell her where the textbook was a bit old-fashioned, and what the more up-to-date way of saying things might be.

Most of all, Louise found it was just nice to have someone to try things out on. 'You get to the stage where you have all these words and phrases going round in your head, and you just need to try them out on a real speaker.'

Louise says, 'Greek was an easy language for me to learn. The alphabet was a bit unfamiliar, but it didn't take very long to understand it. The shapes of the letters were all familiar, even if I didn't know which sound they went with, and I could make a stab at reading right from the very start.

'Some words looked really strange at first sight, but when I worked one out, letter by letter, I'd suddenly find that it was a word I already knew.'

Louise found that Greek vocabulary was also surprisingly easy. English has many words composed of Greek parts, and it was easy to recognise these parts in the words she was learning. 'You use words like telephone and polygon in English without thinking that they've been borrowed from other languages. And you think of words like polygamy or dipsomania as being unusually difficult words in English – words you might find written down, but you perhaps wouldn't use yourself. But in Greek, these bits crop up all over the place in everyday talk. *Poly* is just "very", "much" or "many", and *dipso* is "I drink" in Greek.'

Louise came across so many connections between Greek and English that she thought it would be useful to make a list of them. They fell into two sets. There was a list of about 30 words that often appeared at the beginning of English words, and often corresponded to adjectives or prepositions in Greek. These were things like *amphi* (both), *endo* (inside), *hem* (half), *hyper* (above), *hypo* (below), *iso* (equal), *neo* (new), *peri* (around), *proto* (first), etc. Louise could easily think of English words that contained these bits, and so they were easy to learn. The other set was Greek words that usually appeared at the end of English words. 'Scope' is a good example of this kind of word. You get it in 'telescope' and 'periscope' and 'bioscope' but *scopo* is just Greek for 'view'. *Sphere* is another Greek word that works in the same way. Louise says: 'Learning Greek was completely different from learning any other language. Most of the time, I've found it hard to learn vocabulary, but this time I felt I already knew a lot of the vocabulary before I started. It wasn't so much a question of learning new words, more a question of finding out how many I already knew. It meant that I could often guess how to say something in Greek, even if I wasn't sure what the words were.'

The extra bonus from learning Greek was that it made Louise think a lot about English. 'My little boy is really interested in dinosaurs, and I could never remember their names. But once you find out that the Greek word for "lizard" is *sauros*, *brontis* is "thunder", *ankylos* is "crooked" or "bent" and *stegis* is "roof" or "home", words like brontosaurus, ankylosaurus and stegosaurus stop being difficult, and start to become quite funny instead!'

Because such a lot of basic Greek vocabulary is related to English, it's fairly easy for native English speakers to develop a good passive vocabulary very quickly. Louise wanted to see if this made it easier for her to read Greek.

'When I learned French at school,' she says, 'I tried to read novels with a dictionary, but I always found so many words I couldn't understand that I never managed to read more than a few pages. It really put me off.'

With Greek, she tried a different strategy.

'I bought some Greek books from a second-hand bookshop when we were on holiday,' she says. 'Not Homer or anything like that. These were romantic novels. All the stories were really easy, and even with my basic vocabulary I could make a good stab at reading them.'

Louise used a marker pen to highlight all the words she wasn't sure about. After about 6 months learning Greek, she found that she highlighted about 20 words on each page of her novel. This wasn't a lot, but it was still too much to look them up in the dictionary. Each time she stopped to look a word up, it broke the flow of the story. So instead of stopping each time she found a new word, she'd make a guess at what it meant, but not stop reading. Then, when she'd got to the end of the chapter – usually four or five pages – she'd look up all the highlighted words in her dictionary, and check how close her guesses were.

She was surprised at how good she was. Almost all her guesses were partly correct. Sometimes she was wrong, but quite often the story made it obvious that she'd made a mistake, and she'd be able to backtrack and get it right. Some words were easier than others, of course. Things that the people in the story picked up or did something with were the easiest. For instance, if someone picked up an object and drank out of it, it had to be a cup, or a glass, or a bottle, or a wineskin – the details probably didn't much matter. Or if the heroine was describing the man she had just fallen in love with, she'd be unlikely to say he was stupid, ugly and bad-tempered. She might say something on those lines when she quarrelled with him later, of course, but that was another matter. Verbs were the hardest to guess; Louise could guess the general area easily enough, but often needed to be more accurate than that to understand the story properly. Fortunately, the same words kept coming up again and again, and each time she met one, she got a few more clues to what it really meant.

Louise also noticed that as the story developed it became easier to guess what an unknown word meant, because she was used to the characters and the way they acted. If the villain drove round in an expensive sports car with a gold medallion on his hairy chest, you could be sure that the bulge in his jacket pocket wasn't a pocket bible, even if you didn't know the Greek for loads of money!

Louise says, 'Guessing words when I was reading made it much easier for me to cope with spoken language too. It made me more confident that I could understand something, even when I wasn't sure.'

What kind of a language-learner are you?
Louise found it easy to recognise Greek words because she had a big vocabulary in English. How big is *your* English vocabulary? Try this test and find out.

Read through this list of words, and tick all the ones you think you know. You don't need to be very strict with yourself – if you don't know exactly what a word means, but have a rough idea of how it's used, say 'yes'. You won't know all the words. Twenty of them aren't real words at all. They're there to make sure you don't cheat!

1 clamp	21 humane	41 mingose
2 tepid	22 decrepit	42 hyperbole
3 allifont	23 degrify	43 aconite
4 turbulent	24 primeval	44 killick
5 parminous	25 mensible	45 myopia
6 morsel	26 devoid	46 bosker
7 populous	27 laminate	47 nugatory
8 outpanner	28 lorch	48 acrimony
9 gnarled	29 mercantile	49 bauxite
10 fanfare	30 furtive	50 mangrove
11 mellible	31 objective	51 fellous
12 yolk	32 abrasive	52 jeremiad
13 exclude	33 gillickry	53 fallology
14 ferdic	34 condense	54 latifundia
15 loiter	35 frigory	55 pragmatic
16 estuary	36 logarithm	56 cantry
17 vessey	37 destriptic	57 glyph
18 acoustic	38 didactic	58 motet
19 implex	39 fricassee	59 fricative
20 dabble	40 epitome	60 fulline

How to score your answers

Score 1 point for every word you ticked.

If you ticked any of the words below, take off 2 points for each word:

3	5	8	11	14	17	19	23	25	28
33	35	37	41	44	46	51	53	56	60

What your score means

The higher your score, the bigger your English vocabulary.

The more words you know in English, the more likely it is that you will be a good language-learner. The reason for this is that people with big vocabularies are obviously good at learning words in English, and can transfer these word-learning skills when they are learning a foreign language.

26–40 points

If you scored close to 40 points, you have a bigger than average vocabulary. You probably read a lot; you don't often come across a word that you don't know, but if you do you can usually guess what it means. If you are adventurous, you probably try out these new words for yourself. You might even find that the people you work with comment on the words you use when you talk. You will have no problems learning the vocabulary of a new language, and if you're learning one like Greek, you'll find many words you already recognise from English.

0–25 points

If you scored around 25 points on the test, your English vocabulary is about average. You're not often stuck for a word, but often come across ones you aren't sure of, and you probably don't read for pleasure. Learning a language like Greek won't be particularly easy for you, but you'll probably find that it increases your English vocabulary as a side effect.

Minus points

Lots of minus points? This means that you thought you knew ones that don't really exist. Maybe you deliberately cheated to try to push your score up? If not, you really need to check the words you thought you knew with a dictionary – you'll probably find that some of them actually mean something else. Start with the easy words at the beginning of the test. The ones towards the end are rare ones that you're less likely to know.

Remember

★ An untrained native speaker isn't necessarily a good teacher of a language. Find out what he or she is good at, and get him or her to help you in that area.

★ Don't be put off by writing systems that seem difficult at first sight – they're often much easier than they look.

★ Learning a foreign language can teach you things about your own language. It can also teach you things about the different ways other people think and behave. With 'minority' languages such as Greek (not widely taught and not often spoken by foreigners) the mere fact of trying to speak the language will bring you a lot closer to the people. For some people, that's what learning a language – whatever the language – is all about.

WHERE TO GO FROM HERE

About other languages

It is not possible here to do justice to all the languages in the world which merit study by adult learners in the United Kingdom. How, in the end, do you decide the importance of a language? By size of vocabulary? The number of native speakers? Economic power? Literary heritage? The number of countries where it is spoken? Whether they are prime holiday destinations? The surface area of the country where it is the official language? Its use in international trade? Its simplicity? Its difficulty? Its intrinsic interest?

The following languages are each of interest for different reasons.

Turkish

As Turkey has begun to rival Greece as a prime European holiday destination, so interest in learning Turkish, at least at the 'Get by in . . .' level, has increased.

Turkey itself lies partly in Asia and partly in Europe. The Turkish or Turkic group of languages is spoken by over 150 million people, not only in Turkey but also in Azerbaidjan, Yugoslavia, Bulgaria, parts of Greece and Cyprus. Immigrant workers, especially in Germany and the United Kingdom, account for almost a million more Turkish speakers in Europe.

Since the Turkic languages are not part of the Indo-European family, learners have to cope with a completely new vocabulary, with very few cognates. However, grammar is regular, pronunciation not difficult and, since the reforms of 1928, the script is a modified Latin one.

Malay and Indonesian

Malay is the most widely spoken language throughout Malaysia and Indonesia. The southern Malay dialect has been the official standard language of Indonesia since 1949, under the name Bahasa Indonesian (*bahasa* means 'language') or, simply, Indonesian. It's spoken by about 85 to 90 million people. Malay is an official language for some 160 million people.

There are two scripts: Malay (adapted from Arabic) and a romanised version, which is gaining ground.

Hungarian, Finnish, Estonian

These three European languages do not belong to the Indo-European family, with which we are by now familiar, but to the Finno-Ugrian branch of the Uralic group of languages. As such, they present considerable difficulties for the European learner.

Finno-Ugrian language family.

Korean

Korean, like Japanese, is a relatively isolated language. It is spoken by well over 50 million people in North and South Korea (where it is an official language), China, Japan and the USSR, as well as in large Korean communities outside the Far East.

As trade between Europe and the Far East increases, so too will interest in learning Korean and understanding Korean culture.

Swahili

Africa contains more languages than any other continent. It is also a continent of lingua francas.

★ **English** and **French** are in widespread use, often as official languages in former colonial territories.
★ **Portuguese** is still spoken in its former colonies: Mozambique, Cape Verde and Angola.
★ **Creole** or pidgin versions of English, French and Portuguese are also common.
★ **Arabic** is used in the north and north-east.
★ **Swahili** is spoken throughout most of East Africa, with some four million native speakers. Over 30 million use it as a lingua franca.

If you had to choose one African language to learn, Swahili is perhaps the most useful, especially if combined with both English and French.

Hebrew

Hebrew, like Latin, was for many centuries mainly a written language. The modern spoken and written form is used by about four million people in Israel and throughout the world. With the establishment of the state of Israel in 1948, Hebrew became one of the country's two official languages. The other is Arabic. Like Arabic, Hebrew is a Semitic language.

Esperanto

The 'curse of Babel' and the 'divine confusion of tongues' has led many people over the years to search for an acceptable, artificial 'world' language. Esperanto, invented in 1887, is perhaps the most durable. It draws upon the vocabulary and grammar of the main European languages, and is spoken by its enthusiastic proponents in many parts of the world. It's claimed that roughly five million people speak some Esperanto, but it still remains a long way from challenging English as an international language.

Selecting a course

Materials

You've decided which language you want to study. When browsing through your local bookshop, trying to choose a course book and/or audio cassettes, apply the following criteria:

★ Is the price right? The cheapest course may not match up to your expectations – it may not be thorough enough or take you far enough in the language. There may not be as much explanation or grammar as you need, or enough chance to practise structures and patterns. On the other hand, it may be just what you want to make a start before investing time and money in a more ambitious course.

Equally, the most expensive course may not necessarily be the best, or the best for you. There may be too much material, or the course may proceed at too fast a pace for your own particular needs and interests. If, however, you seriously want to master the language in question you may find a solid, complete set of materials more satisfying than a short course which doesn't take you far enough.

★ Most course books have an introduction, but most people don't bother to read it – until it's too late! Instead of buying a course book on the strength of the blurb on the back (which, after all, is designed to persuade you to buy the book) do read the introduction – there's every chance that this will give you a good idea of whether or not the book will suit you. It will clarify the structure of the book, the amount of time you can expect to spend on study and what you should be able to achieve by the end of the course.

★ Check the contents page. If the chapter headings include titles such as: 'The subjunctive', 'The pluperfect tense', 'Comparatives and superlatives', or 'Fricatives and sibilants', the chances are it's either very old-fashioned or designed with a particularly scholarly or analytical learner in mind. Chapter headings which suggest themes, or uses to which you can put the language (such as 'Asking the way', 'Saying what you'd like', 'Buying things', 'Talking about yourself') are likely to be more relevant to your needs.

Beware also of headings like 'At the chemist's', 'At the railway station', or 'At the market'. These may suggest a situational approach to language which, though sometimes helpful, doesn't always take account of the need to transfer patterns from one situation or context to another.

★ Check the cultural content. A course with very little, or even no, cultural content is only half a course. Getting to know the culture of the country is as important as learning its language. In the best courses the two go hand in hand.

Classes

If you have the opportunity to attend a day or evening class near you, you'll probably find the experience of learning a foreign language more enjoyable and more satisfying. Classes usually begin in September, and it's worth checking them out with your local authority, college, polytechnic or library well in advance, before the most popular languages get booked up! It's a good idea to delay your choice or purchase of a major course book until you find out which one the class teacher plans to use. It's also worth checking at your nearest university – they frequently run 'extramural' or continuing education courses for adult learners at all levels.

Now you've gone so far along the road to finding out how to learn a language, we hope you'll be going further still. The list of addresses and contacts that follows is designed to help you do that. You may find it useful to go back over some of the key sections in the book ('How do languages work?' (p. 43), for instance, and the 'Remember' sections at the end of each chapter). These will remind you of some of the things to bear in mind while you are learning your language. Most of all, though, we hope that you'll be going forward to an enjoyable and successful experience, **'learning the lingo'**.

GOING FURTHER

If you need more information about learning languages in general, try contacting:

CILT (Centre for Information on Language Teaching and Research), Regent's College, Inner Circle, Regent's Park, London NW1 4NS. Tel: (071) 486 8221.

CILT has an excellent library on all aspects of languages and linguistics. They also operate an enquiry and publicity service, and regularly publish books and other materials on the teaching and learning of languages.

For more specific requests or information about particular languages, and courses in those languages, in this country or abroad, try the following:

French: Institut Français, 17 Queensberry Place, London SW7 2DT. Tel: (071) 589 6211.

German: The Goethe Institute, 50 Princes Gate, London SW7 2PH. Tel: (071) 581 3344.

Spanish: Instituto Cervantes, 102 Eaton Square, London SW1W 9AN. Tel: (071) 235 1484.

Italian: L'Istituto Italiano di Cultura, 39 Belgrave Square, London SW1X 8NX. Tel: (071) 235 1461.

Russian: The Great Britain-USSR Association, 14 Grosvenor Place, London SW1X 7HW. Tel: (071) 235 2116.

Japanese: 1. Information Centre, Embassy of Japan, 101–104 Piccadilly, London W1V 9FN. Tel: (071) 465 6500.
2. The Japanese Language Association, Bath College of Higher Education, Newton Park, Bath BA2 9BN. Tel: (0225) 873701.

Welsh: Canolfan Iaith, Nantgwrtheyrn, Caernarfon, Gwynedd LL53 6PA.

For other minority languages within the European Community contact the European Bureau for Lesser Used Languages, 10 Sráid Haiste Íocht., Baile Átha Cliath (Dublin) 2, Ireland. Tel: 353 1 612205/618743.

For other languages, the embassy of the country concerned should be able to advise you. Ask for the cultural attaché.

Most of the main languages also have their own professional associations, which can advise on materials, classes, courses, study groups, visits to the country by groups or individuals, etc. These associations may be approached in the first instance through the parent organisation:

ALL (Association for Language Learning), 16 Regent Place, Rugby CV21 2PN. Tel: (0788) 546443.

The **Central Bureau for Educational Visits and Exchanges** offers information on all kinds of educational visits and exchanges. These include study visits and short courses abroad for teachers, programmes to encourage an awareness of Europe in schools, and programmes for students, such as work-placement schemes. In addition the Bureau publishes a number of guides to working, studying or simply living abroad. These include *Working Holidays*, a guide to over 99 000 paid and voluntary opportunities in over 90 countries world-wide; *Study Holidays*, a guide to learning European languages in the countries where they are spoken; and *Home from Home*, a guide to home stays and exchanges.

All of these offer opportunities to practise, improve and brush up your language skills. The bureau's address is: Seymour Mews House, Seymour Mews, London W1. Tel: (071) 486 8221.

For information on the tests, examinations and qualifications that are available for language-learners, try contacting one of the following:

RSA Examinations Board, Murray Road, Orpington, Kent BR5 3RB. Tel: (0689) 32421.

London Chamber of Commerce and Industry, Marlowe House, Station Road, Sidcup, Kent DA15 7BJ. Tel: (081) 302 0261.

Institute of Linguists, Mangold House, 24a Highbury Grove, London N5 2EA. Tel: (071) 359 7445.

The Institute of European Education, Graded Testing Unit, St Martin's College, Lancaster LA1 3JD. Tel: (0524) 2423.

Cambridge University Local Examinations Syndicate (also known as UCLES), Syndicate Buildings, 1 Hills Road, Cambridge CB1 2EU. Tel: (0223) 61111.

If you have a specific business, industry or company-related language-training requirement you should try contacting your local branch of the nationwide network of **Language Export ('LX') Centres**. They exist to identify, and provide for, the language-training needs of business and industry in their area, and can organise individual or group training according to demand. They can also devise tailor-made language-learning packages.

The Secretariat of the Association will put you in touch with your local or regional LX Centre: PO Box 1574, London NW1 4NJ. Tel: (071) 224 3748.

The **Open University** has established a Centre for Modern Languages, with plans to offer language-teaching courses and materials in its undergraduate and continuing education programmes, beginning with French, followed by other European languages such as German and Spanish, and, eventually, non-European languages such as Japanese and Arabic.

For further details contact: The Director, Centre for Modern Languages, Walton Hall, North Spur Building, Milton Keynes MK7 6AA. Tel: (0908) 653834.

Radio and television

The *Radio Times* contains current details of all BBC radio and television language programmes. Further information about the content, broadcasting and forward planning of BBC language programmes, and associated publications, can be obtained by writing to: **The Education Officer for Modern Languages**, BBC Education, BBC White City, 201 Wood Lane, London W12 7TS. Tel: (081) 746 1111.

The World Radio and TV Handbook (published by Billboard Books) is a useful guide to what's on on the world's air waves: which country broadcasts on what frequency at what times and in which languages. You'll find it (or you can order it) at your local bookshop.

GLOSSARY

adjective Adjectives are words like 'good', 'stupid', 'happy', etc., that can be used to describe nouns. Not all languages have adjectives – in some they are just a special type of verb. In some languages, adjectives always come in front of the noun they describe, but in many they have to come after it. Adjectives in your language may change depending on the *gender* and *number* of the nouns they are describing.

adverb English words that end in 'ly' are adverbs. Some languages don't have them at all or, at least, they don't have a special adverb form and use an ordinary adjective instead. If your language does have adverbs, the odds are that they are made up by adding a special ending to an adjective. Watch out for languages like German where there are special rules for where an adverb has to come in a sentence.

article Articles are words like 'the', 'a' and 'an' in English. 'The' is sometimes called the 'definite article'. 'A' is sometimes called the 'indefinite article'. Watch out for:

★ languages which don't have articles at all, or languages which have definite articles but no indefinite ones.
★ languages where the articles come after the nouns they go with, instead of in front as in English.
★ languages which have different articles depending on the *gender* of the noun they go with.
★ languages where the articles change shape depending on the *number* of the noun they go with.

case Case is the term used in old-fashioned grammar books to describe the different jobs that nouns can do in sentences. The main jobs you have to describe are: the *subject* of a sentence (who or what did it?) and the *object* of a sentence (who or what was it done to?). You may find that nouns in your language change their form depending on which of these roles they play in a sentence.

Case is a real problem for English speakers – on the whole, nouns don't change their form in English when they take on a different role in a sentence.

If your course book uses these terms, and you find them hard, try switching to a book that uses a different methodology. You don't need to be a grammarian to speak a language.

cognates Cognates are words from two different languages which look very similar, and mean the same sort of thing. Languages which are closely related usually share lots of cognates, and this sometimes makes them easy to learn. For instance, if you're learning Dutch, you find that *huis* is 'house', *muis* is 'mouse'. What do you think *luis* is? In German, they'd be *Haus*, *Maus* and . . .

Not all words that look like cognates actually are: some look as though they ought to be cognates, but are actually *false friends*. The Dutch word *tuin*, for instance, doesn't mean 'town', it means 'garden'. And some words that were originally cognate have changed their meaning in one of the languages. For instance, *embarazada* in Spanish is the same as our word 'embarrassed', but in modern Spanish it means 'pregnant'.

conjunctions Conjunctions are words like 'and', 'but', 'if', 'moreover', 'because'. Their main job is to join short sentences together to make longer, more complex ones.

consonant Don't confuse consonant sounds with the letters we usually call consonants in English (B, C, D, F, G, H, J, K, L, M, N, P, Q, R, S, T, V, W, X, Y, Z). Consonants are sounds that you make when you block the air coming out of your mouth instead of letting it flow freely.

dialect Someone once said that a language is a dialect backed up by an army and a navy.

Most languages have standard forms, which tend to be used on radio and television broadcasts. Learners are usually taught standard forms, and examiners will usually expect you to speak this. In real life, many of the native speakers you meet won't speak the standard form. All languages vary a lot, not just in the way they are spoken, but also in their grammar. Some linguists have suggested that languages don't really exist – rather, there are groups of people who speak dialects that are quite close to each other, and don't present real communication difficulties.

dictionaries There are two main types of dictionary: *bilingual* dictionaries give you lists of words in two languages; *monolingual* dictionaries give you lists of words and their definitions in the same language. You can also get picture dictionaries.

Most learners buy a dictionary and are disappointed because the words they need aren't in it. There are three reasons for this. First, languages contain thousands and thousands of words, and you can't fit them all into a small book. Fortunately, many of them don't crop up all that often, and so most dictionary-makers economise by concentrating on more common words. This means you are very unlikely to come across technical terms for engineering or computing in a small pocket dictionary. It is possible to get hold of specialist dictionaries, but they are often very expensive. If you really need a technical one, try your local library or chamber of commerce. If you belong to a professional organisation, it might also be able to help.

The second reason is that a lot of vocabulary appears and disappears very quickly, and often doesn't get the chance to be recorded in a dictionary. Think of a word like 'bonking' – it probably wasn't widely used before 1985 or so, and won't appear in any dictionary published before that date. It probably won't still be around in 2001.

The third reason for problems with dictionaries is that a lot of technical vocabulary is very recent. For example, terms like 'byte' and 'integrated circuit' were not in common currency 10 years ago, although they are very much part of modern everyday language. Dictionaries don't change very often, and it is difficult to keep up with changes like this. Bilingual dictionaries are often based on already existing monolingual ones, and so they lag even further behind. The smaller the dictionary, the worse its coverage will be: bilingual dictionaries often have a very small number of entries.

In general, it's not worth buying a very small dictionary, especially if you're interested in recent usage. More often than not, one that contains less than 10 000 words will let you down. On the other hand, most learners don't need a huge multi-volume tome, which they would need a magnifying glass to read. A dictionary that contains 30–40 000 entries will be adequate for most learners' purposes.

etymology Where a word comes from, and how it is related to words in other languages.

false friends *see* **cognates**

gender Nothing to do with *sex*. Many languages divide their nouns into different types which are usually referred to as genders. French and Spanish, for instance, have two genders: masculine and feminine. German has three: masculine, feminine and neuter. These names are very unfortunate, because they suggest that it all has something to do with sex; we expect masculine nouns to have something to do with men, feminine nouns to have something to do with women, and neuter to cover the rest. As a general rule, the link with sex sometimes works. Unfortunately, however, it doesn't work all the time, and you end up with all sorts of odd cases.

Gender generally has its roots in the way the language was spoken hundreds of years ago. In Spanish, for instance, the two genders we have today are a simplification of five different types of nouns in Latin.

Genders are a real problem for English speakers, mainly because of other things that go along with them. In languages that have genders, articles and adjectives tend to change depending on the gender of the nouns they describe. In Spanish, you'd say '*el caballo blanco*' (the white horse), but '*la vaca blanca*' (the white cow). Not all languages are as simple as this, though. However, there are some short cuts to learning genders and the features with which they are associated. Sometimes, you can tell the gender of a word by looking at its ending. In Spanish, masculine words usually end in '-o' and feminine nouns in '-a'. With other words that don't fit this pattern, it helps if you learn them as part of a phrase, rather than on their own. For instance, don't just learn *pared* (wall). Learn *una pared blanca y alta* (a high, white wall) where the **-a** ending on *una* and *blanca* and *alta* tells you that *pared* is feminine.

Does it matter if you make mistakes in genders? It all depends. If you're doing an examination, the examiner might give you low marks if you get them wrong. In real life, gender mistakes don't much matter. You might sound a bit funny if you consistently get them wrong, but people won't often misunderstand you. You're better off making a guess at a gender and making a mistake than coming to a complete halt in mid-sentence.

grammar Grammar is a way of describing the way languages work. Traditional language courses spent a lot of time explaining grammar, and a lot of time practising grammatical exercises to make sure you got it right.

Grammatical terminology is useful because it helps you put labels on the regular patterns in a language. You don't need a lot of it, but you'll find it useful to know how to recognise a *noun*, a *verb* and an *adjective*. Other terms are explained in this glossary, but you can manage without them.

idiom An idiom is a phrase or expression peculiar to a particular language. Translated literally, word for word into another language, it usually becomes meaningless. It may, however, have an equivalent in another language, expressed in different images or words. Idioms are part of the colour and personality of a language. Learn a few of them, and you'll give added value to your own linguistic ability. Keep your ears open for phrases that are often used by native speakers of your language, and try to use them in your own speech. They make you sound incredibly fluent, for very little effort.

How to make fun of someone in several languages:

★ You're pulling my leg (English)
★ *Me tomas el pelo*: You're taking my hair out (Spanish)
★ *Tu me fais marcher*: You're making me walk (French)
★ *Mi prendi in giro*: You're taking me around (Italian)

In English (and in other languages) feet feature frequently in idioms. If you're going to learn a language, you have to stand on your own two feet. If you don't, you might get cold feet, or even put your foot in it. However, if you put your best foot forward, you're unlikely to put a foot wrong. You may even find your feet, and finally be able to put your feet up!

inflection Some words change their forms depending on the other words that they are linked to in a sentence. These changes are called inflections. In Indo-European languages, they are usually found at the end of a word, and are sometimes referred to as endings for this reason. Not all languages work in this way. Some don't have any inflections. Watch out, too, for languages like Arabic where the endings are less important than the changes that take place in the middle of words.

intonation The way your voice goes up and down when you speak. Most languages have very characteristic intonation patterns, and you can make your pronunciation sound much more authentic by imitating them closely.

language laboratories Language laboratories vary in size, shape and make, but basically they consist of a library of tapes and cassettes and a number of individual listening and recording booths where you can play the tape of your choice in private, or under the controlled supervision of a tutor or native speaker. You can choose just to listen, or to listen to and repeat or otherwise respond to, the material on the tape. In most laboratories you can also record your own voice and, using an instant playback facility, compare it with the voice of the native speaker on the tape.

The language laboratory has the advantage that you can work at your own pace, you can make mistakes in private and you can record your own voice without inhibition, comparing it with the model on the tape. If you can't always spot the difference, your teacher or a native speaker will be able to help. Above all, this is a good way to develop your self-confidence – and that's terribly important at all stages of language-learning, particularly at the beginning.

Many colleges have language laboratories, and some allow members of the public to use them for a small charge.

lingua franca A language that is widely used in a particular area, even though it probably isn't the mother tongue of the people who speak it.

minilab A Minilab is a special kind of cassette player that allows you to do some of the things that you can do in a full-size language laboratory. The main feature is that you can listen to the taped lesson on one track of the tape, and record your own voice on the other at the same time. You can then play both tracks back together, and compare your own efforts with the model on the tape. Minilabs are rapidly becoming standard equipment in up-market self-tuition courses.

newspapers and magazines Whatever stage of language-learning you're at, it's really useful to browse through newspapers and magazines in the language that you're studying. Of course, at the beginning you won't understand very much, and it will be a long time before you understand everything. However, because you're familiar with the context of some news stories, or have visual support from photographs, designs and graphic layouts, you'll be surprised at how much you can guess.

Browsing helps you to:

★ reinforce what you already know
★ recognise cognates
★ learn new words
★ meet authentic language
★ develop your guessing skills
★ learn up-to-date idioms and vocabulary
★ practise your ability to decipher different scripts

noun Nouns are words that name something. All languages have nouns, but they behave in different ways in different languages. Use this check-list for the language you are learning, to see if you can expect to have problems with nouns.

★ Some languages have more than one type of noun (see **gender**).
★ Some languages have nouns that change their endings when you have more than one object (see **number**).
★ Some languages have nouns that change their endings depending on what role the noun plays in a sentence (see **case**).

number Almost all languages make a distinction between one and more than one, and show this by changing the form of a noun when it means more than one. Grammar books use the term 'singular' for one item, 'plural' for more than one. In English, for instance, we say 'cow' and 'cows' – though we also have 'sheep' and 'sheep'. In Indo-European languages, this change is usually an alteration at the end of a word. Other languages use other methods: for instance, in Malay, you say a word twice to show that you mean a plural.

Some languages have a special form for two items.

In some languages, if you use a numeral (three, four, five, etc.) you have to use the singular form of the noun.

parts of speech An old-fashioned way of referring to different types of words. The traditional parts of speech are: *nouns, pronouns, verbs, adjectives, adverbs, prepositions* and *conjunctions*.

phoneme A technical term that you might meet in some courses designed in the 1960s and 1970s. A phoneme is a set of different sounds that can be regarded as the same when you are talking about a particular language. For instance, in English 'l' and 'r' are different sounds, but in Japanese they are pretty much interchangeable. In Japanese, 'l' and 'r' are members of the same phoneme.

Phonemes are important because they explain why learners find it hard to develop a good accent. You tend to hear a foreign language in terms of the phonemes of your native one, and this can make it hard for you to hear sounds that your own language doesn't use.

phonetics The details of the way a language is pronounced. (People often use 'phonetics' when they mean *phonology*.)

phonology The sound patterns of a language. In theory, languages could use any combination of sounds to make up their words, but in practice it doesn't work like that. The sounds a language uses tend to fall into patterns of similar sounds. For instance, if a language has a 'v' sound, it's very likely that it will have an 'f' sound as well; if a language has a 'z' sound, it will almost certainly have an 's' sound as well. Experienced linguists get to recognise these patterns, and this makes it easy for them to learn good pronunciation.

plural see **number**

politeness Some languages use special forms of words in order to show politeness (or insult) to someone. In some languages, it's also polite not to go straight to the point that you want to talk about, but to approach it gradually in a roundabout fashion. This is something you can only learn from prolonged exposure to your language – but your teacher might be able to give you clues about what to watch out for.

> The Japanese word *hai* is usually translated as 'yes', yet may be better rendered as 'Yes, I'm listening,' or 'Yes, I follow,' or 'Please go on.' This distinction has lulled many a foreign businessman into disappointment and disillusionment with seemingly devious or inscrutable Orientals, who appear to be agreeing but are merely signalling the fact that they are listening!

prepositions Words like 'to', 'of', 'on', 'in', 'behind', etc. in English.
    Watch out for:

★ Languages where prepositions are actually *postpositions*, i.e. they come behind the noun they go with, instead of in front of it. Postpositions crop up a lot in languages where the verb comes at the end of the sentence. (Japanese is a good example.)
★ Languages where the work done by prepositions in English is done by case endings instead. (Finnish is a good example.)

pronouns In English, words like 'I', 'me', 'you', 'they' are pronouns.
    Watch out for languages where it's usual to leave pronouns out. For instance, in Spanish, *canta* can mean: 'he sings', 'she sings', 'it sings' or even 'you sing', depending on the context. Watch out, too, for languages that have special polite pronouns: French *vous*, German *Sie*, Italian *lei*, Spanish *usted*.

punctuation Punctuation conventions are different from one language to another – even between languages that use Roman letters. For instance, the way you report what somebody says differs according to whether you are speaking English, French, German or Spanish. (Have a look next time you find a novel in one of these languages.)

When we see one of these: ?, we know a question's being asked. And when we ask a question (at least in print) we expect to see one too. But not all languages make use of the question mark in this way.

A Spaniard will expect to see two of them, one at the front and one at the end of the question, the first one upside down and back to front:

¿Que tal? How are you?

A Greek will expect to see: ;

Ti eenai avto; What's that?

For a Japanese the word *ka* indicates a question. No need for any question mark at all:

Kore wa nan desu ka What's this?

And that's in romanised Japanese. When the Japanese write in their own characters (*kanji*, *hiragana* and *katakana* – p. 88) there are no spaces between words or sentences.

radio If you have a good radio receiver, you might be able to get programmes in the language you are learning. Many countries broadcast ones specially aimed at learners, and broadcasting companies will often send you information packs, magazines and stickers if you contact them.

The best way to find out about broadcasts in the language you are interested in is to get a copy of the *World Radio and Television Handbook* from your local library. Make sure it's the current edition. Transmission times and frequencies change from year to year.

right hemisphere The brain is divided into two halves, called hemispheres. It's been known for a long time that your left hemisphere (the one on your left-hand side) is more likely than the right one to deal with language. (This explains why people who have strokes in their left hemisphere are likely to lose their speech.) Your right hemisphere is better at handling pictures, faces and music – anything that needs to be processed holistically rather than separately. Your right hemisphere can handle language in its own way, and some people have suggested that you can learn foreign languages more effectively by using these right-hemisphere skills.

sex Nothing to do with *gender*. Some languages have special forms that have to be used if you are a man, and others that have to be used if you are a woman. Arabic and Japanese are good examples of this. Ask your teacher if you think your language might be one of these.

short-term memory About 20 years ago, psychologists discovered that there was a special kind of memory that played an important role in the way we understand and process speech. Short-term memory is what enables you to listen to someone talking, and make sense of what he or she says: you store the sound waves in your head long enough to identify the words spoken and how they relate to each other. Short-term memory is strictly limited in size, so you have to make it work effectively. Non-native speakers often show short-term memory problems in a language. For example, if you ask them to listen to a list of words in their own language and repeat them back, most people can manage seven or more words. Doing this in a foreign language is much harder: you might only be able to manage to repeat back a list of three or four words in a language you are not really fluent in.

singular see **number**

stress In languages where words are often more than a syllable long, you generally find that one syllable is pronounced more strongly than the others. For instance, we say **Eng**lish, not Eng**lish**. Watch out for languages where stress is completely regular. In Finnish, it's always the first syllable that's stressed. In Italian, it's almost always the next to the last one. English is unusual in not having regular stress.

syllable A syllable is a sequence of sounds centred on a vowel sound. 'Cat' has one syllable, 'catalogue' has three.

Syllables in English can be quite complicated.'Strength', for instance, is one syllable but is made up from six different sound segments: 's', 't', 'r', 'e', 'ng' and 'th'.

Watch out for languages where syllable structure is very simple, and each vowel is accompanied by only one or two consonants at most.

tense All languages have ways of showing that actions are taking place at different times, and many do this by changing their endings. The main tenses are the past, the present and the future, but most languages have subtle variations on this. For instance, in English, 'I will learn Chinese' is a bit different from 'I will have learned Chinese' and 'I would have learned Chinese'.

There's no way of avoiding learning the forms if your language is one where tense is complicated. You can probably get away with a few simple ones if you are only trying to get by, but more serious learners will have to learn them by heart. You'll find it helps to learn the forms in a context, rather than spending hours learning tables of verbs.

Lots of 'difficult' languages (for example, Japanese) actually have very regular patterns when it comes to tenses and, once you've recognised how they work, it's not difficult to transfer them to new words.

tone Some languages use different pitches to distinguish between words that would otherwise be identical. These languages usually have short words, and simple syllable structures, and often make questions by adding a word to a sentence, rather than by variations in intonation patterns.

verb Verbs are words that show the relationship between things or people that do something, and the things or people they do it to (see **case**).

Some languages have special rules about where verbs can come in sentences. The hardest ones for English speakers are languages where the verb comes right at the end of the sentence.

Verbs, like nouns, tend to change their shape a lot, and you may have to spend a lot of time learning the ways in which the verbs in your language change, and what makes them change. Traditional grammar called this 'conjugation'.

Things that might make verbs change their form are:

★ Whether the subject is singular or plural (see **number**).

★ Whether the action is taking place now, or some other time (see **tense**).

★ Whether the verb is a command, a wish, a negative or some other form that's not a straightforward description.

You might also find that the verbs in your language fall into two or more different types, which all 'conjugate' in different ways. Most people find these conjugations really difficult at first, but, after a while, they become second nature and automatic, and you won't have to worry about the complications very often once you get more fluent.

Remember, though, that irregular words are often the most frequent items you'll find in a language (think of 'be' in English). Most languages get more regular the more you learn of them.

vowel Don't confuse vowel sounds with 'a', 'e', 'i', 'o', 'u', the letters that are used to represent vowel sounds in English. They can be represented by any letter – for instance, the vowel sound '-oo-' is written '-w-' in Welsh. Most languages have more than five vowel sounds, and have to use a whole range of complicated combinations of letters to show which one is intended. In English, for instance, 'a' sounds different in 'rat' and 'rate'.

Watch out for languages like Arabic where vowel sounds aren't written at all.